ARIEL DORFMAN

Ariel Dorfman is a Chilean expatriate who has made a second
home for himself in the United States. Author of plays, film-
scripts, short stories, poems, essays and novels, including
Widows and *Konfidenz,* he is a Distinguished Professor at Duke
University in North Carolina. His most recent plays, co-written
with his eldest son Rodrigo, are *Mascara* and *Who's Who.*
He has just published a memoir, *Heading South, Looking North:
a Bilingual Journey.*

A Selection of the Other Volumes in This Series

ARIEL DORFMAN

The Resistance Trilogy

Widows
Death and the Maiden
Reader

with an Introduction and Afterwords by the author

NICK HERN BOOKS

LONDON

A Nick Hern Book

The Resistance Trilogy first published in Great Britain
as an original paperback in 1998 by Nick Hern Books Limited,
14 Larden Road, London W3 7ST

Widows, revised for this edition with a revised Afterword,
copyright ©1997, 1998 by Ariel Dorfman

Death and the Maiden translated from the Spanish original
La Muerte y la Doncella by Ariel Dorfman

Death and the Maiden and Afterword
copyright © 1990, 1994 by Ariel Dorfman

Reader, revised for this edition with a new Afterword,
copyright © 1995, 1998 by Ariel Dorfman

All three plays were first published in individual editions
by Nick Hern Books

The right of Ariel Dorfman to be identified as the author
of these works has been asserted by him in accordance with
the Copyright, Design and Patents Act, 1988

Typeset by Country Setting, Woodchurch, Kent TN26 3TB
Printed in England by Athenaeum Press Ltd,
Gateshead, Tyne and Wear

ISBN 1 85459 369 2

A CIP catalogue record for this book is available from
the British Library

Contents

Foreword

My writing has been haunted, ever since I can remember, by twin obsessions, a central paradox that I cannot be rid of: on the one hand, the glorious potential and need of human beings to tell stories; and, on the other, the brutal fact that, in today's world, most of the lives that should be telling those stories are generally ignored, ravaged and silenced.

My life has been fortunate, inasmuch as I have been able to dedicate my existence to reaching others through my imagination; and unfortunate because a great part of that life, like the life of so many others in this twentieth century of ours, has been spent under the shadow of innumerable tyrannies that thrive by denying people the possibility of communicating with each other.

The three plays in this book are part of the continuing exploration of these two opposite experiences of liberation and domination, a conflict, on stage and in history, between these two possibilities whose final outcome we still do not know, can only guess at, a resolution that humanity is still trying to determine.

This inevitably double origin of my work – the dramas as well as poetry, essays and novels – confronted me with a dilemma when the time came to collect my theatre pieces in a single volume: how to call this trilogy, under what name should I mark and celebrate my quest?

I might have placed an emphasis on the different and converging ways in which the State in our sad age punishes those who have rebelled and warns others who have not yet done so to be wary of trying: torture in *Death and the Maiden*; disappearance in *Widows*; and censorship in *Reader*. But to call this *The Repression Trilogy* or *the Violence Trilogy* or *the Trilogy of Abuse and Suffering* would have been to miss what I hold to be most central to my writing: that it tries to place, hopes to place, in the very middle of history those who do not accept life as it has been established and narrated, the wager that the official version of reality handed down from above will always be contested by somebody, no matter what the cost to their bodies and sanity. It is their rebellion, our rebellion, which sets in motion the crisis which is at the heart of each play: Paulina will not forget or let society forget what has been done to her; Sofia will not allow her men to be left without burial or memory; Tanya will come back from the dead to shadow the husband who betrayed her and force him to admit the life he has suppressed. If I have to unify the plays under a single banner, it is, it must be, that of *Resistance*.

That all three rebels I have mentioned happen to be women is not, of course, a mere coincidence. Because women often tend to be the least powerful, the most marginal, members of society, when they do revolt, they do so with a determination, fury and dignity which cracks the world open, which compels authority to reveal itself in all its arbitrary ugliness. But women have also fascinated me because – and this may be why I have gravitated towards them as a detonating factor over and over – their very lack of influence makes their insurrection extremely precarious. In order to prevail, they need to convince the men who hold power to change their conduct, they need to invade that masculine world and throw it into chaos, they need their version and view and gaze to be validated and verified and accepted. The plays do not, therefore, merely tell the story of the women who set history upside-down, but also of the men whose history is being directly challenged: the Captain and the Lieutenant, in *Widows*; Gerardo and Roberto, in *Death and the Maiden*; and particularly, Daniel Lucas and Alfonso Morales, in *Reader*.

If I have divided these men thus, into pairs, one and one, one and the other, either/or, it may be because that is how they came to me, dramatically, or perhaps because it was a way of recognising the two jagged sides to each dominant issue, the inevitable division I see splitting the inside eyes of those who command, the alter egos and altering egos of the men I somehow tend to create, I am besieged by these male figures who know, often in spite of themselves and against their better judgment, that they are the incomplete mirrors of somebody else. Men who desperately want to stop repressing others. Men who know that if they stop repressing others, they will lose the violence that centres and cements their identity.

I look at these plays again, knotted together here for the first time, I look them over one more time and I see yet another characteristic that unifies them: they are all mysteries that do not have a solution. Is the Doctor guilty of the horrors he is accused of in *Death and the Maiden*? Where are the bodies that appear in the river in *Widows* coming from? Who, in *Reader*, is narrating the secret story of Alfonso, of Daniel, the story that only one person in the world really knows? The ambiguity of the final solutions in each play is directly related to the freedom I have wanted my readers and spectators to experience, the certainty that the story on that stage has not yet, in fact, ended, that how it really ends will depend on how we, who are watching, act out our own lives. And that writer's confidence in the imaginary and its strength to transform the spectator is paralleled inside the dramatic world itself by the ferocious pull of the imagination on the protagonists, male and female, the way in which they are cornered, they have cornered themselves, into conceiving another alternative, a different possibility, for humanity.

If I have written that word, *ferocious*, it is because the imagination is never entirely benevolent in the worlds I have invented. It is, indeed, often destructive. Paulina's imagination is what allows her to keep her dignity through years of solitude and self-loathing; but it is also what may have betrayed her, constrained her to accuse a man who may be innocent. The protagonist's imagination, in *Reader*, is the one glorious, subversive, resurgent element of his conscience which will not let him continue censoring himself or the world; but it is also what drives him to madness and, ultimately, death. Sofia's imagination, in *Widows*, is her howling instrument against death, what helps her to conjure bodies from the river and refuses to let the loved ones be burnt like garbage; but it is also what will lead her to sacrifice her life and her family's.

If the imagination cannot triumph completely in these three plays (nor in my two more recent ones, *Mascara* and *Who's Who*, written with my eldest son and collaborator, Rodrigo), if the derelict moral order cannot be fully restored, it is not for lack of trying on my part. There is nothing I would like better than to have each of these tragedies culminate in a just society, a magnificent burial, the disappearance of censorship and guilt. I would love my protagonists to live at peace, to have found the benign closure to which they aspire and which – who knows? – they may even deserve. That this is not the case may be due to human nature – or may perhaps be due to something that we might some day remedy: the limitations that power and history objectively place upon rebellion, aesthetic and political, in our times.

I have suffered those limitations, witnessed them, in the country
that is at the core of these three plays, that inspired them, that
brought them to life: Chile. Torture, disappearance, censorship –
and above all rebellion, are not faraway experiences that I have
added to the sauce of my work in order to enliven it: this is what
has constituted this life of mine for far too many years and that
even now, when the dictatorship is over and we are negotiating
an arduous transition to democracy, continues to visit and
damage every citizen of my country.

Yes, Chile is what forced me to write these plays. To make
sense of what it meant to live in a time when life could be
snuffed out – just like this, with the snap of a finger, the snap
of darkness.

Though it is not only about Chile that I write.

A long time ago, a few years after General Pinochet had taken
power, as I watched my country being ravaged from afar,
watched the arms and legs of the country being pried open,
every word of the country being violated, a long time ago,
I decided that this suffering could only be justified if we were
able to turn it into something else. Not necessarily to learn from
it. Rather to grow with it and from it, to make it significant,
to rise from defeat. To punish with words the men we cannot
punish with other means. To prove that we had not suffered
in vain. That some of us might have the last word – if not the
last laugh.

And from that determination – and the need in exile to communicate with those who had no idea of where Chile lay and did
not much care to know either – sprang the final distinction that
I believe joins all three plays: they could all transpire in many
places, they have been quite deliberately conceived as trans-
cending the immediate circumstances of their fiery birth.
Not that they cease to be marked by the history that violently
brought them into being. Not that I am repudiating their origin
in a small land at the end of the earth which is still paying the
moral consequences of what some of our citizens did to others,
the pain and disappearance and erasure of words and bodies.
I will never deny that we should always refer my characters
back to the real men and women who inspired me to make up
these stories. And yet, my incarnations speak, have spoken in
many languages, to many nations beset by similar problems,
communities which ask themselves how to deal with a world
where women cannot bury their men, where a solitary fractured

human being in a remote beach-house cannot get one person in the universe to believe the eternal injury done to her, where an old bent man tries to suppress the story that reveals his hidden sins to the son he loves.

These events did not happen only in Chile. They did not even happen there primarily. They happen on every stage in every country, and now, with this book, inside every reader, anyone who dares to share my voyage of hope and fear, the voyage of trembling and hope of my plays, the voyage that goes on and on and perhaps will not easily die.

Ariel Dorfman, January 1998

WIDOWS

Characters

THE FUENTES FAMILY
SOFIA FUENTES, *the Grandmother*
ALEXANDRA, *married to her son Emiliano*
YANINA, *married to her son Alonso*
FIDELIA, *daughter of Alexandra*
ALEXIS, *son of Alexandra*
ALONSO, *son of Sofia*

THE WOMEN OF THE VALLEY
TERESA SALAS
KATHERINA
ROSA
MARILUZ
AMANDA
LUCIA
RAMONA

CECILIA SANJINES, *girlfriend of Emmanuel, the Orderly*

PHILIP KASTORIA
BEATRICE KASTORIA, *his wife*
KASTORIA'S BROTHER

FATHER GABRIEL, *the parish priest*

THE ARMY
THE CAPTAIN
THE LIEUTENANT
EMMANUEL, *the Orderly*
THE DOCTOR
SOLDIERS

*There can be fewer valley women, and there can be many
more. The minimum number is three. The minimum number
of non-speaking soldiers is two. Some parts may be doubled:
Beatrice Kastoria can be played by a valley woman, as can the
Brother, since he isn't seen. One actor can play The Doctor,
Father Gabriel and Philip Kastoria – and perhaps Alonso.*

ACT I

Scene 1

The WOMEN *by the river, washing clothes.*

TERESA. The baby won't speak?

YANINA. Not a word.

TERESA. He's how old?

YANINA. Old enough to talk.

KATHERINA. Good that he's quiet, he'll stay out of trouble.

TERESA. He has to talk sometime . . .

KATHERINA. Not if he knows what's good for him.

ROSA. There's something wrong with the water today.

ALEXANDRA. You say that every day.

ROSA. Nothing's coming clean.

MARILUZ. Whisper to him.

ALEXANDRA (*to* ROSA). You just don't scrub hard enough.

MARILUZ. Whisper. Right in his ear.

KATHERINA. That baby misses his papa.

YANINA. He never saw his papa.

Little pause.

FIDELIA. I'll whisper to him.

TERESA. Work his tongue with your fingers, a little each day.

YANINA. Fidelia tells him stories.

ALEXANDRA. Instead of doing her chores.

FIDELIA. Mama . . .

ROSA. There is. There's something strange about the water today.

YANINA. He's a sad baby.

KATHERINA. You think he knows that his papa is . . .

TERESA. Ssshhhh . . .

YANINA. He knows what I know.

A little pause, then FATHER GABRIEL *enters, breathlessly.*

FATHER GABRIEL. Everyone come, it's time, it's time!

He exits.

CECILIA (*entering*). The jeep just pulled up. The new captain's here . . .

The WOMEN *stare at* CECILIA. *An icy silence.*

CECILIA. It's a big jeep.

She exits.

The WOMEN *put down their washing, wring dry wet things, load everything into baskets and, whispering to each other, exit.* SOFIA *is left alone, sitting by the river.* FIDELIA *re-enters.*

FIDELIA. Grandma, don't you want to see . . . ?

ALEXANDRA *re-enters dragging* ALEXIS.

ALEXANDRA (*to* ALEXIS). Stay with your Grandma.

ALEXIS. I want to see the new Captain. I want to see what he looks like.

ALEXANDRA. I don't want him to see what you look like. I'm a smart woman. Why did I have such stupid children? Fidelia . . .

FIDELIA. Grandma, they said this Captain – he's bringing news. Don't you . . .

ALEXANDRA. Fidelia, come. (*To* SOFIA). You've turned everything upside down. The others think you've gone crazy and my children don't listen to me now.

ALEXANDRA *and* FIDELIA *exit. A little pause.* ALEXIS *looks at the silent* OLD WOMAN, *who watches the river expectantly.*

ALEXIS. Grandma . . . ?

Are you crazy?

SOFIA. Yes.

ALEXIS. When did you go crazy?

SOFIA. Do I scare you?

ALEXIS. No.

SOFIA. Little rabbit.

ALEXIS. I'm not. I'm a man.

SOFIA. Not yet. Lucky.

The CAPTAIN *enters, on foot, following a surveyor's map;
under his arm, plans and designs in plastic tubes.*

CAPTAIN (*to* ALEXIS). You, boy, can you tell me if . . .

ALEXIS *runs away.*

Come back here, I . . . damn.

(*To* SOFIA). Excuse me, Mrs . . . uh . . . I'm trying to . . .

SOFIA *shows no sign of being aware of his presence.*

Is this the bend where the women do their washing? (*Picks
up a piece of clothing.*) Must be.

I thought it would be greener.

We're going to build here. Big plant. For fertiliser
manufacturing.

The OLD WOMAN *mutters, shifts her skirts.*

What? Did you . . . Are you from around here, your
husband, does he ever talk about fertiliser? Well, I think you
just have to look at how arid it all is, to see . . . it's poor soil
nutrients, that's why . . . Does your husband ever express
the need for modern fertilisers for his land?

SOFIA. No.

CAPTAIN. Oh. Well I think fertiliser would . . . help. The
army's going to build a plant here, then he'll see what he's
missing. Your husband. Bigger crops. Exports. Are you . . .
What are you doing here? Are you waiting for someone?

SOFIA. Yes.

CAPTAIN (*introducing himself*). I'm . . .

SOFIA. I'm waiting for my father.

CAPTAIN. Your father.

SOFIA. And my husband.

CAPTAIN. How old is your father?

SOFIA. And my sons.

CAPTAIN. Your father must be at least . . .

SOFIA. Old.

CAPTAIN. Been waiting long?

Little pause. She looks at him.

SOFIA. The others. They all ran off to the village. To have a look at you.

She laughs, a small, dry, sly laugh. It makes him uncomfortable at first, then he gets it, and he laughs too. Then she stops laughing.

All of us. We have all been waiting a long time.

Scene 2

The CAPTAIN *and* EMMANUEL.

EMMANUEL. Did you find the bend in the river, sir?

CAPTAIN. Of course I did. I can read a map. And the river's not exactly a mystery to follow.

EMMANUEL. I'm supposed to drive you, sir, that's my job.

CAPTAIN. I'll let you know what your job is, Orderly.

EMMANUEL. Yes sir.

CAPTAIN. When I want to walk, I'll walk. Understood?

EMMANUEL. As you say, sir.

CAPTAIN. Good. You're from around here, aren't you?

EMMANUEL. On the other side of the hill, Captain. Forty miles from here.

CAPTAIN. So you understand these people?

EMMANUEL. Sort of, Captain.

CAPTAIN. Sort of. Captain Urqueta said you knew your way around.

EMMANUEL. I'm different from them, Captain. I was employed by Mr. Kastoria, I know better. With your permission, sir, I don't think I'll stay here my whole life. I'd like to . . .

CAPTAIN. I met an old woman. Tough old bitch. By the river. I got the impression she was expecting someone on a . . . raft, or something . . .

EMMANUEL. Old Sofia. The Fuentes woman.

CAPTAIN. You know her?

EMMANUEL. She sits by the river all day, sir. Has for months. Probably a little . . . (*Indicates 'crazy'.*) She told you she was waiting for her men?

CAPTAIN. I could barely get a word out of her. Her father and her husband and . . .

EMMANUEL. Her sons. A lot of the men in the valley are . . . they're gone, sir.

CAPTAIN. Gone.

EMMANUEL. Disappeared, they . . .

CAPTAIN. Arrested?

How many men in all are missing?

EMMANUEL. All, sir.

CAPTAIN. All? *All* the men?

EMMANUEL. I . . . think you should speak to the Lieutenant, sir.

CAPTAIN. *All* the men? That wasn't mentioned in the briefing. (*Pause.*) In my other jurisdictions I kept a lid on that – making men vanish like that – it's no good. It drives the women out of their minds. Even if you give them a finger to bury, but when there's just nothing . . . They go crazy. And then the world does.

Hard times.

EMMANUEL. Yes sir.

CAPTAIN. She has a little moustache.

EMMANUEL. Sir?

CAPTAIN. I hate women with moustaches.

(*Looking out the window.*) Her whole family?

EMMANUEL. All the men.

CAPTAIN. I suppose then we'll have to forgive her . . . her moustache. Won't we?

FATHER GABRIEL (*entering*). We're glad you finally made it, Captain. We'd heard you were lost.

CAPTAIN. Who told you that, Father?

FATHER GABRIEL. Oh, in Camacho we end up knowing everything, Captain. But the women are waiting.

CAPTAIN. Women waiting. We don't want that.

Scene 3

The CAPTAIN *is addressing the* WOMEN. *He is alone on stage and talks to the audience.*

CAPTAIN. The war is over: in the cities, in the mountains, in this valley. What remains is the national task of building a deep and true peace, the peace that brings prosperity. But in the memories of some, the war goes on.

Terrible, strict measures have been necessary; we have all suffered great loss, the people and its army.

Those of us with determination and courage for the future are ready to let go. We are ready to forgive your disobedience if you are willing to forget our stern response to it, if you learn to behave. If you join us, if you are prepared to forget the past, the wounds may finally begin to heal. Democracy and technology will be brought to bear on your backwardness, fertiliser plants and animal husbandry, pesticides and . . . and libraries; a new land for a new people. And if you let us, we will bring your sorrow and great loneliness to an end.

Scene 4

SOFIA *at the river, alone.*

SOFIA (*to the river*). What are you bringing me? I'm an old woman. I can't be expected to wait much longer.

FIDELIA *enters running.*

FIDELIA. They're coming home, they're coming home!

ALEXANDRA (*entering*). Sofia, where's Alexis?

Little pause.

Sofia? Where's . . .

SOFIA (*dazed, looking about*). I don't know, he was here, he must have gone home.

ALEXANDRA. Oh Sofia, you were supposed to watch him.

FIDELIA. I thought he was supposed to watch her.

ALEXANDRA. Quiet. ALEXIS! (*She exits, calling his name.*) ALEXIS!

FIDELIA. Papa's coming back, grandma, everyone's excited, they . . .

TERESA *appears, shucking corn. She's there but not there.*

TERESA. Fidelia, don't tell lies.

FIDELIA *stops, looks at her, then:*

FIDELIA. I'm not lying, the new captain, he said the men are coming . . .

TERESA. He said maybe. If we behave . . .

KATHERINA (*appearing, mending clothes*). If we behave.

    YANINA *enters*.

FIDELIA. But we behave already, all we do is behave, we . . .

TERESA. Sofia doesn't.

KATHERINA. Sitting by the river all day . . .

TERESA. She doesn't behave.

YANINA. Take the baby, my arms are tired.

    YANINA *gives the baby to* FIDELIA.

ALEXANDRA (*calling off*). ALEXIS!

YANINA. You should have come, Sofia, the new captain met with us, he spoke to us, he said . . .

TERESA. Forget the past.

KATHERINA. Bury the past.

ROSA (*appearing, stirring a pot*). Let go the dead.

TERESA. He didn't say that.

KATHERINA. He never mentioned the dead.

YANINA. He promised us, Sofia, if we co-operate, he said . . . maybe we can't trust him, if you'd been there, you could tell us, if you'd seen him . . .

SOFIA. I saw him.

ROSA. Listen to her, she lies worse than her granddaughter.

SOFIA. Mind your business . . .

ROSA. It is my business, he said behave.

SOFIA. He said fertiliser plant. I know what he said.

YANINA. But you were here the whole time. How, how did you . . . ?

SOFIA. Go home, Yanina, it's almost dusk, put the nets on the baskets or the grasshoppers will crawl out of the ground and eat the grain.

YANINA. I did that already.

FIDELIA. I helped her, grandma, we . . .

SOFIA. You probably did it wrong. You put the nets on all anyhow and the grasshoppers slip through.

KATHERINA. Full of advice, criticising everyone, but she hasn't worked in a month. Give yourself some advice, Sofia, act your age . . .

TERESA. Sitting there . . .

ROSA. Like a river rock . . .

KATHERINA. Stubborn, bitter, a tombstone . . .

ROSA. Reproachful . . .

TERESA. As if to say that we've forgotten the . . .

ROSA (*crossing herself*). Sssshhh.

TERESA. That's why you can't brood. You'll lose your mind, you'll turn to stone.

ALEXANDRA (*still off*). ALEXIS!

ROSA. When they took the land away from us, and we had to watch the fences go up again, and . . . and smile. You whispered to me, like a promise, Sofia, life goes on, like the earth, no matter what. Now get up.

SOFIA. I can't. I'm carrying the weight of my four men. I have a father. Husband. Two sons. Where? Each one is heavy. Each time I think of him, is he hungry, does he need water, is he cold, he gets heavier. I am a stone. Where are they? Where are my men? I remember the missing so sharply I've forgotten everything else, how to bake or plant or walk or even stand. I can't move. I'm waiting here because . . .

ALEXANDRA *enters, dragging* ALEXIS.

FIDELIA. Grandma? Because . . . ?

SOFIA. I'm waiting. Because I can't bear waiting anymore.

ALEXANDRA. I'm tired of this. We're going home.

FIDELIA. Grandma.

ALEXANDRA. Leave her. On the ground there like an animal. (*To* SOFIA.) They're watching and you know it. You call attention to yourself. To all of us.

ALEXANDRA *begins to exit with* FIDELIA. ALEXIS *tries to stay behind to talk with* SOFIA.

ALEXIS (to SOFIA). I had to run, mama told me not to let . . .

ALEXANDRA *pulls* ALEXIS, *they leave with* YANINA *and* FIDELIA. SOFIA *sits alone. All the* WOMEN *disappear except* TERESA.

SOFIA. Don't you feel something . . .

TERESA. Feel what?

SOFIA. Something is coming.

TERESA. No.

SOFIA. Something is.

Little pause.

TERESA. When my husband comes back, he'd better find me tending the fields and feeding the children and selling the crops at market. I wait too, but not like this, Sofia, not like this.

She exits.

SOFIA (*puts her hand in the river*). Something is. It's almost here.

Scene 5

CECILIA *and* EMMANUEL *by the river; he's trying to make love to her.*

CECILIA. Not here.

EMMANUEL. I love this place. Green.

CECILIA. I hate green.

EMMANUEL. Even before I knew you, this place reminded me of you. I knew someday I'd be here with you.

CECILIA. I used to come here with . . . (*She stops.*)

EMMANUEL. Say who.

CECILIA. Let's go.

EMMANUEL. Theo. (*Calling, teasing her.*) Hey, Theo!

CECILIA. Stop it.

He's coming back. Everybody says . . .

EMMANUEL. Stupid bitches.

CECILIA. The captain told them. I heard him.

EMMANUEL. He never said . . .

CECILIA. All the women, they're getting their beds ready . . .

EMMANUEL. Then there are going to be a lot of disappointed women in cold beds around here – except for one little sweet woman I know. She's luckier . . .

He gropes her, she pulls away.

CECILIA. Those witches. They hate me because we're in love. They'll tell Theo.

EMMANUEL. You're protected.

(*Grabbing his uniform.*) You know what this is?

(*Grabbing his pistol.*) You know what this is?

What's he got? Your husband? Even if he did come back he won't but say he did? See those trees?

CECILIA. Yes.

EMMANUEL. I love those trees. Try to touch the fruit on those trees someone you don't even see will shoot your hand off. Green Kastoria land. Protected. When I was a kid I'd come here, I'd walk six hours, I watched for. birds.

CECILIA. Did you climb over and steal the fruit?

EMMANUEL. Not me. I watched for the birds, if they tried to land in the fruit trees, I threw pebbles at them and scared them off. I knew even then I was supposed to protect his property – that that was what I was born for. Mr. Kastoria didn't know I was alive and if I'd climbed over the fence they'd've shot me but I was proud to be protecting what was his.

My father used to beat me. He knew where I'd been and when I got back he beat the shit out of me.

CECILIA. Poor baby.

EMMANUEL. Do you know what a war is?

CECILIA. I know what a war is. Yes.

EMMANUEL. You take sides and if you lose, you're fucked. 'They stole the land from our people.' That's what he said when he beat me with the belt, 'they drove us into the mountains,' he said and he'd belt me, 'now we have to come and pick their fruit,' and he would . . . He was right to beat me. My father knew I was his enemy.

One day I just didn't come back. Mr. Kastoria rode out of the gate on a big white horse and asked me if I wanted to work for him. Know what he said?

CECILIA. No.

EMMANUEL. He said, 'You've got to shoot the birds that eat the fruit. That way they won't come back.' And he handed me a gun. My father must have waited for me all day, with his strap in his hand, watching the horizon. I never went home again.

The CAPTAIN *and the* LIEUTENANT *standing atop a hill nearby.*

LIEUTENANT. You know what I love about this country, Captain? Its quality of timelessness. One man is born a peasant, over there, in the dust, and his son will be and his son will be, and if you allow it there's a deep satisfaction, a calm, that comes from that. And on this side, the green fertile side, the transfer of property through the generations. My father and his father and his father . . . The Fourteen Families: for four hundred years we have cultivated a loving relationship to the land, gentle and subtle, making it produce for all. There is a deep, an inevitable structure in the world, a Holy Structure, if you will. So it is also inevitable that the people of the dust will always covet the green; if they get ideas, feel encouraged to lay hold of the green, everything, everything decent and beautiful and civilised, gets covered in dust. As we have seen in the last eight years.

CAPTAIN. And you are telling me this. . . ?

LIEUTENANT. Back in town with the women yesterday,
I don't mean any disrespect, Captain, but that was a very
nice speech you made. Democracy. Fertilisers.

CAPTAIN. I'm getting into the habit of making speeches. I'm
good at it.

LIEUTENANT. It was a very nice speech. Of course not the
speech I'd've made. If I was Captain. But I'm not.

CAPTAIN. But if you were . . . you'd have spoken of. . . dust?

LIEUTENANT. In a way. I'd've said: 'Congratulations. You're
alive. Want to stay that way?' Captain. We can't give the
impression we're weak.

Pause.

CAPTAIN. Lieutenant, back in Chipote, a few years ago, I
ordered my battalion to fire on a crowd in the village
square. I stood and watched that. When it was dark I took
my flashlight and I searched among the bodies in the
square. There was so much blood it seeped into my boots.
There was a nine year old kid. So young. His arm was . . .
You know. I stood there and watched him die. It took an
hour. The boots dried while I watched. And then the
flashlight burnt out.

Weak men die from nights like that. I'm not a weak man.
But . . . I am tired. The war is over.

LIEUTENANT. Over.

You see down there by that bend in the river. Looks like a
flyspeck, but it's an old woman.

CAPTAIN. Old Mrs. Fuentes.

LIEUTENANT. You think . . . it's over for her? Go on, tell her
that. Just be sure you're carrying a gun.

It's taken us eight years to restore order. And it's our duty to
ensure that we never have to restore order again. So you
never have to watch a little boy die like that ever again. So
I never have to watch what I have watched.

CAPTAIN. No order without progress.

If you want to keep order you have to pull them out of their poverty, their dust. We have to move forward.

LIEUTENANT. And you will wind up right back here again. Looking at the green, at the dust, at that old woman. Timelessness. The past awaits you, Captain.

CECILIA. Times are changing, Emmanuel. Maybe we could go see your family. Make it up with your father.

EMMANUEL. He . . . He's a loser.

Doesn't matter.

CECILIA. Why not? It matters to me.

EMMANUEL. They took him. Disappeared. Like Theo. And he's never coming back.

Scene 6

Late at night at the riverbend. SOFIA, FIDELIA and ALEXIS.

SOFIA. Here, where the river thinks of going one way and then goes another – this is where they died.

ALEXIS. Who killed them?

SOFIA. You know this story.

FIDELIA and ALEXIS. Tell us again, Grandma.

SOFIA. The Spanish. My great-great-great grandfather and his wife. She was fierce. The Spanish believed she ate the eyeballs of her enemies . . .

FIDELIA. Did she?

SOFIA. I hope so.

I light these candles for their little souls. This water saw them die. The water watches everything, it flows everywhere, and when I am lost, or when I've lost something, I know the water will help me find it. You have to know how to ask it.

She strikes a match, lights first one candle, then another.

Now these little souls will watch over me, and you go home to bed. Go my babies, if your mother wakes up and finds you missing . . .

In the surrounding darkness, a lit candle is seen – it appears to float.

ALEXIS. Grandma, is that . . .

SOFIA. Sssshhh. Who is that? Who's there?

The river grows more audible.

TERESA (*entering*). I can't sleep at nights with you here, all I do is watch you . . .

SOFIA. You live miles from here . . .

TERESA. From the window, by my door . . . I heard the floorboards creak and it was Antonio. I thought it was Antonio, it's the same dream, every night since you started sitting here, it's my husband, but he won't talk to me, and it's you, Sofia, you're disturbing him, wherever they've got him, go home, let me rest.

KATHERINA. (*entering*). I heard Roberto calling out to me and I ran out the door to greet him and the yard was empty and I saw these candles. I want to sleep, Sofia, without dreaming. Leave the night alone.

SOFIA. I have dreams too.

I can see my hand, and in my hand there's a needle and a thread, and I'm sewing something, I look down to see, and it's a mouth I'm sewing, I'm sewing it shut, and it's eyelids I'm sewing, and human ears, all familiar somehow, and there's no blood on the needle and no blood on the thread and on my fingers it's . . . and I've sewed him into a bundle, a tight white bundle, he's calling to me, I hear him, I fear he may be dead but oh God let him be alive.

The sound of the river grows terribly loud. ROSA *enters.*

ROSA. What's wrong with the water, what's wrong with the river, why is it making such a terrible noise, what have you done, Sofia, what are you doing to the water in the river? You're clouding the river, the clothes won't come clean, leave the river alone . . .

FIDELIA. Grandma, what is it, what's the matter with the river?

TERESA. There's something in the water, there's something in the water, get a line, get a hook . . .

ROSA. The children, get the children away from the . . .

SOFIA. Alexis, Fidelia, get away from the river . . .

The WOMEN *begin to wade into the river; the sound of the current grows louder still. The* WOMEN *whisper the following, or maybe we hear it whispered urgently on tape:.*

TERESA. Careful careful, don't slip, he . . .

ROSA. Grab the sleeve, grab the . . .

SOFIA. On the rocks, he's caught on the rocks, pull, pull . . .

TERESA. Pull, pull . . .

SOFIA. Now lift. Gently.

The WOMEN, *soaking wet, pull the body from the river. Immediately the sound of the current softens, grows calm.*

SOFIA. Ooohhhh. I knew it.

Silence. MARILUZ *enters. Behind her, the other* WOMEN.

MARILUZ. Oh God. Oh God it's not . . .

TERESA. It doesn't look like anyone.

SOFIA. I knew, I knew . . .

ROSA. Children don't look. Sofia, it's not . . . It hasn't got a face.

Pause.

SOFIA. Fidelia, go get the priest. And bring a shovel.

ALEXIS. Who is it, Grandma?

SOFIA. It's my father.

TERESA. It's not your . . . It isn't, Sofia.

SOFIA. It is.

TERESA. You can't bury that.

SOFIA. Not here. He has a place, by my mother. In the cemetery on the hill.

ROSA. You need permission.

SOFIA. Not for this.

TERESA. The captain said behave.

AMANDA. For God's sake, Sofia, you know you need
    permission.

LUCIA. We can't make trouble now.

ROSA. They have our men.

FIDELIA. Grandma, if Papa were. . . if my Papa. . .

    Pause.

SOFIA. No trouble. Yes. Permission.

    It is my father.

    She starts to leave.

ALEXIS. Wait. I'll go with you.

    Pause.

SOFIA. Aren't you afraid?

ALEXIS. No.

SOFIA. You should be.

    Come.

ROSA. You can't take the boy, are you out of your . . .

FIDELIA. Grandma, mama will be angry if . . .

SOFIA. This is how it should be. His father would accompany
    me. Emiliano. If he was here. This is how the Fuentes bury
    their dead.

KATHERINA. The Fuentes should protect their children.

SOFIA. No one can protect him anymore.

    Fidelia. No one touches this body. You understand?

FIDELIA. Yes, grandma.

SOFIA. Alexis, come.

    Nothing to fear. This Captain is different. Right?

TERESA. You'd better hope so.

SOFIA. *You* hope. I'm going to bury my father.

They exit. The remaining WOMEN *watch the body.*
YANINA *enters.*

YANINA. I woke up, I couldn't sleep, I . . .

She sees the body.

Oh. Oh. Oh God.

Little pause.

Who?

Scene 7

Very early dawn. The doctor stands near the river, smoking.
The WOMEN *in a group, near the body. The* LIEUTENANT
enters with soldiers.

LIEUTENANT. Full of surprises, this river. I don't suppose
anyone's moved the body, right?

Pause.

Yes or no?

The WOMEN *shake their heads no.*

And which one of you found it?

The WOMEN *make an inclusive gesture; they all found it.*

DOCTOR. He's dead, no doubt about it.

LIEUTENANT. I was hoping you could provide us with more
specific information, Doctor.

The DOCTOR *gestures to a soldier, indicates how he wants*
the body turned. The soldier turns the corpse over.

(*To* TERESA.) You found the body?

Pause.

Answer. Did you find it?

TERESA. Yes sir. Along with the others, sir.

LIEUTENANT. Recognise it?

TERESA *doesn't answer. She looks at the body. The*
LIEUTENANT *turns to* AMANDA.

Did you look at his face?

AMANDA *shakes her head, backs away.*

I asked you a question. Jesus Christ, were you people born
deaf?

(*To the* DOCTOR.) Take the pants off.

DOCTOR. This is only a preliminary . . .

LIEUTENANT. It'll help to identify him.

RAMONA. We didn't want to.

LIEUTENANT. You didn't want to see his face?

RAMONA. No sir.

LIEUTENANT (*to the* DOCTOR). Take off the goddamn
pants.

Pause. The soldiers take off the corpse's pants.

So?

DOCTOR. Burns, contusions, broken bones – a disaster. It
looks to me like he was given a good beating before they
dumped him in. He was hungry too. Look at these ribs.

LIEUTENANT. I think the river is responsible.

DOCTOR. For the burns?

LIEUTENANT. I don't see burns. Look closer.

DOCTOR. I already told you what I think. But if you think
differently . . .

LIEUTENANT. Any clues about the subject's identity? Age?

DOCTOR. I can't tell the age. He seems to have been away
from the sun months, years perhaps. A peasant. Look at
those hands – of course they're broken now, the . . . river,
I suppose.

LIEUTENANT. And in the pockets?

DOCTOR. Nothing.

LIEUTENANT (*to the* WOMEN). You women. I want you to pass by this body, one by one, and take a good look at the face. A formal identification process.

Everything nice and proper for the new citizens of the new land.

The WOMEN *do this, except* FIDELIA.

KATHERINA. It could be my brother, sir. They took him away four years ago.

LIEUTENANT. Your brother? Are you sure? (*Pause.*)

KATHERINA. How could I be sure? How could I want this to be my brother?

LIEUTENANT. I wouldn't want it to be mine.

Good. The people have spoken, or rather not spoken.

He gestures to soldiers to cart the body away. When they move towards it FIDELIA *goes right to the body.*

LIEUTENANT. Well well. Re-enforcements . . .

FIDELIA. It's my great-grandfather.

The LIEUTENANT *looks at her in a frankly sexual way for a long time.*

TERESA. Ignore her, sir, she's a little strange.

LIEUTENANT. Your great-grandfather. Oh my. And what's your pretty name?

FIDELIA. Fidelia Fuentes.

LIEUTENANT. Emiliano's daughter?

FIDELIA. Yes. This is my great-grandfather. Carlos Mendez.

LIEUTENANT. And you identified him just like that, girl, from a distance?

FIDELIA. My grandma Sofia identified him, sir.

LIEUTENANT. Strange she's not here. We didn't think grandma could move. We thought she was screwed to the spot.

And where might she be now? Would you happen to know that?

Before answering FIDELIA *moves hesitantly to the corpse, sits beside it, and takes one of its hands in hers.*

FIDELIA. She went to the captain, sir. To ask permission to bury her father.

LIEUTENANT. She's wasting her time.

Pause.

Now get away from that body.

Pause. FIDELIA *doesn't move.*

Don't fuck with me, girl.

Pause. The LIEUTENANT *and the soldiers watch* FIDELIA, *who doesn't respond, doesn't move. The* WOMEN *stand at a distance, but not too far.*

TERESA. Leave her be, sir. I told you she's strange.

YANINA. Fidelia, come.

LIEUTENANT. You're the wife of . . . Alonso, right? I'm good at remembering names.

YANINA. Fidelia!.

FIDELIA. My grandma never wastes time, sir. She doesn't believe in that.

The LIEUTENANT *goes to* FIDELIA, *grabs her by the shoulders, picks her up with great strength but complete control, and moves her away from the body. He kisses her violently, lets her go. Then he motions to the soldiers. They pick up the body, carry it out.*

DOCTOR. I need a drink.

LIEUTENANT. There's the river. Don't fall in.

He exits. The WOMEN *remain, immobile.*

Scene 8

The CAPTAIN*'s office, the* CAPTAIN, EMMANUEL, SOFIA *and* ALEXIS.

CAPTAIN. You're sure about this.

SOFIA. Yes.

CAPTAIN. This drowned man is your father. You're sure?

SOFIA. Yes.

CAPTAIN. Why would an old man like that have gotten mixed up with politics?

SOFIA. He didn't.

CAPTAIN. Well, you said he was arrested. For what?

SOFIA. For nothing.

CAPTAIN. Mrs. Fuentes, people don't get arrested for nothing, they . . . (*To* EMMANUEL.) Emmanuel, did you know this man? Mendez.

EMMANUEL. Yes sir.

CAPTAIN. Well . . . ?

> *Little pause.* EMMANUEL *very uncomfortable under* SOFIA*'s stare.*

CAPTAIN (*slightly impatient*). Orderly?

EMMANUEL. Mendez, her father, went around to houses and churches and places where the men would drink and . . . talked about land. Mr. Kastoria's land. He was angry when we . . . moved them off the land. Fuentes her husband also. First and mostly her father. The files say he is no longer in custody.

CAPTAIN (*to* SOFIA). Perhaps you're confused.

SOFIA. No.

CAPTAIN. Perhaps your father ran way, or . . .

SOFIA. No.

CAPTAIN. He might have had an accident, or . . . well, sometimes men run away for . . .

SOFIA. He could barely walk.

CAPTAIN. Women make men do strange things.

SOFIA. He was eighty years old.

CAPTAIN. Or sometimes terrorists have business to settle amongst themselves . . .

SOFIA. No, he wasn't a violent man. He wasn't a . . .

CAPTAIN. Well he must have been doing something. Stop interrupting me.

He reaches in his desk, takes out a sheet of paper.

This is the new amnesty decree. Do you know what amnesty is? Am-nes-ty. If your father or your husband . . .

SOFIA. Or my sons.

CAPTAIN. Or whoever. Has been in trouble with the government, now they can surrender. Without inconvenience. So maybe they'll come back to you from wherever they're hiding. What would your father think if he came back and found you burying him? Hmm?

She picks up the paper, examines it like a strange object, turning it over and over, and then putting it back carefully on his desk.

SOFIA. I've come for permission to bury my father.

CAPTAIN. Yes, yes we established that, we know that, you said that already, now have you heard a single word I . . .

SOFIA. He came to me . . . from the land of the dead. His body. Because he wanted me to bury him. Where all the dead of our family are buried. In the cemetery on the hill. He came back to his daughter for that. Give me permission.

There is a knock on the door. The LIEUTENANT *enters.*

LIEUTENANT. I'd like to speak with you for a moment, sir, if . . .

CAPTAIN. Of course, I . . . Lieutenant, you know Mrs. Fuentes? And this is her grandson . . . mmmm . . .

LIEUTENANT. Alexis.

CAPTAIN. Alexis. Right.

Mrs. Fuentes, I'm a reasonable man. Pending the results of the official inquest, this body, if it can be established that it really is your father . . .

SOFIA. Carlos Mendez.

CAPTAIN. If it is . . . Carlos Mendez, then you will naturally be allowed to bury him. The army is the servant of the people.

SOFIA. I'll wait.

CAPTAIN. It may take . . .

SOFIA. I'll wait.

SOFIA takes ALEXIS by the hand and exits. The CAPTAIN snaps his fingers at EMMANUEL, who follows them out.

CAPTAIN. She never blinks. Crazy old bitch. Makes me nervous. After the inquest . . .

LIEUTENANT. Inquest.

CAPTAIN. Give her the body. Quickest way to get rid of her.

LIEUTENANT. You're joking.

Inquest? Give her the . . . You're joking.

CAPTAIN. I don't think I am.

LIEUTENANT. And what do we do after the funeral?

CAPTAIN. After the . . . ?

LIEUTENANT. When she wants to know: who killed him.

Little pause.

No evidence.

CAPTAIN. What do you mean, no . . .

LIEUTENANT. No evidence.

CAPTAIN. Where's the body, Lieutenant?

The LIEUTENANT picks up a pinch of ash from the ashtray, blows it into the air.

LIEUTENANT. Gone.

CAPTAIN. You . . .

LIEUTENANT. Burned it.

Sorry.

CAPTAIN. You . . . You *burned* the . . . How dare you, how fucking *dare* you, I gave you orders to bring that corpse back to . . . You BURNED it? That is a flagrant violation of my orders, of proper military procedure, you . . .

LIEUTENANT. What are you talking about? Excuse me, sir, but what are you . . . Proper military . . .

Listen to yourself. Somewhere right now somewhere else in this country, maybe your last command, someone is losing a piece of paper, erasing a signature, burning a body to cover your ass. And you . . . cover mine. That's how the army's going to survive in your new democratic paradise. I cover you, you cover me.

CAPTAIN. You killed him? Her father? You . . .

LIEUTENANT. I arrested him.

CAPTAIN. And you . . .

LIEUTENANT. Let him go the next day. What happened after that . . . is not for us to say.

CAPTAIN. Mother of God. You burned the . . .

What do I tell her? That old bitch out there with that stupid kid, for Christ sake, what do I say to her?

LIEUTENANT. Say there's no body. Say there never was a body. Say 'Fuck off you old bitch'.

The CAPTAIN *goes to the office door, opens it, sees the old woman sitting outside, and closes the door.*

CAPTAIN. She's waiting out there.

LIEUTENANT. Don't tell her anything.

CAPTAIN. Well I can't just . . . let her wait. She'll wait forever.

LIEUTENANT. Not forever. She's an old woman. You'll probably outlive her.

End of Act I.

ACT II

Scene 9

ALEXANDRA *and* YANINA *are pounding grain,* FIDELIA *pouring it into sacks.*

ALEXANDRA. Pour it slower, you spill half on the ground.

FIDELIA. I'm not spilling anything.

ALEXANDRA. Don't talk back to me.

YANINA. You're spilling, Alexandra, you're pounding too hard, half of it's coming over the sides . . .

ALEXANDRA. I can't believe she took Alexis. (*To* FIDELIA.) I can't believe she left you to guard that thing. I can't believe you touched it, you're so dumb, it's unclean. Did you wash your hands? Did you wash your mouth?

FIDELIA. You asked me already, I said I did, stop yelling at me, I . . .

ALEXANDRA (*overlapping with above*). I can still smell it, I don't think you washed enough, you'll get that death in the grain, I . . .

YANINA (*overlapping with above*). You'll wake the baby, please stop . . .

SOFIA *and* ALEXIS *enter.* ALEXANDRA *immediately stops talking and begins pounding even harder.* ALEXIS *heads for the house.*

ALEXANDRA (*to* ALEXIS). You. Stay.

Little pause. Pounding.

SOFIA (*to* ALEXANDRA; *very tightly controlled rage*). You're pounding too hard. (ALEXANDRA *pounds even harder.*) You'll crack the bowl, stop pounding so . . .

ALEXANDRA. Don't. Talk. To. Me.

SOFIA. That bowl you are breaking is my bowl and I won't let you . . .

ALEXANDRA. Nothing here is yours, it's yours if you work it and you, you haven't done any work in a month, and now it isn't yours any more, it's mine, my bowl, my house, my goat and chickens and grain and . . . and MY children and you . . . just go back to the river and leave me and what's mine, all the things you don't care for anymore!

SOFIA (*very quiet*). There were four goats when I left a month ago and now there are only three. How much did you get for Cholito?

ALEXANDRA. You know what I can't forgive? It's not disgracing your father's name by giving it to a rotting corpse, it's not being a crazy old woman who can't help herself because crazy old women can't help the way they are, what I cannot forgive, ever, is that you . . .

SOFIA. I asked you a question.

ALEXANDRA (*barely controlling herself*). What.

SOFIA. How much money did you get for the goat?

ALEXANDRA (*quietly*). You put my daughter and my son in danger . . . I thought . . . the one thing I could depend on was that you cared about my children. Your grandchildren. That you would protect them. You care about nothing but death.

FIDELIA. No, mama, that's not true, she . . .

SOFIA. Fidelia. What did I tell you when I left you at the river?

FIDELIA. Grandma, I . . .

SOFIA. I entrusted you with the body of my father. And you let those godless men take my father's body and they burned it, like trash, and you let them do that.

ALEXANDRA. Don't talk to my daughter like . . .

SOFIA. She should have died before she let them take his body away! Forgive! I don't forgive any of you for that!

(*To* ALEXANDRA.) You have no Mendez blood in your
veins, no Fuentes blood, you don't understand, but you (*To*
FIDELIA.) I thought you were Emiliano's daughter, but you
understand nothing, none of you, I come back and you're
going to market, my father's body, he built this house, black
smoke and ash and you're going to market, you'll sell the
living, you'll sell the dead, nothing's horrible enough to
stop your selling, and your pounding, any of you, any of
you in this whole valley, you bitches, you whores, you sell
the lives and the memories of your men, you should all be
down like stones by the river, you should all be tearing your
clothes by the river, the sun and the moon and the wind
should stop till you bury the dead, I will, I'll find where
they burned the corpse of my father and I'll gather his ashes
and the earth that they scorched and I'll carry it to his grave
on the hill, you'll see that I will, every ash, every splinter,
you'll see that I will, and then maybe you'll stop, and then
maybe you'll see: This was my father, and where is Miguel,
and this was my father, and where's Emiliano, tell me, tell
me, where is your husband, and this was my father, and
where is Alonso, Yanina, tell me, Alonso, Antonio, where's
Theo, where's Luis, where's Raul, Pablo, Hernando,
Claudio, Joaquin, where is Juan, Enrique, Luis, Rafael,
Pablo, Armando, Benito, Felipe, Sebastian, Theo, Joaquin,
Miguel, Miguel, Miguel, Emiliano, Alonso, Diego, Flaco,
where are you, Federico, Ricardo, Eduardo, Saul, Andres,
Carlos, Lorenzo, Gabriel, Cristian, where's Segundo, David,
Julio, where's Felipe, Angel, Miguel, Roberto, Mario,
Ernesto, Salvador, Ernesto . . .

She continues to repeat the names, over and over.

THE WOMEN (*as* SOFIA *lists the names*). Not the names,
stop, not the names they'll hear you, they'll hear, no names,
no more, no more, not one more name, they can hear, they
can hear don't say the names, don't say it, don't say it,
don't say . . .

They chant this over and over as ALEXANDRA *says:*

ALEXANDRA (*as* SOFIA *and then the* WOMEN *chants the
names*). Get the grain, get the grain, we're going to the

market, Fidelia, get the sack, Alexis, the cart, Yani, get the
baby, close up the pen, don't listen don't listen, just get the
sack and the cart and . . . YOU CRAZY OLD WITCH
YOU GIVE THEM NAMES, YOU GO TO THEM AND
YOU TELL THEM NAMES, FUENTES, FUENTES,
MENDEZ, YOU GIVE THEM OUR NAMES, YOU CALL
ATTENTION, YOU'LL KILL THEM ALL, YOU'LL KILL
THEM ALL, don't you understand old woman they've got
our men . . .

Little pause.

My husband is not dead! Emiliano is not dead. No!

FIDELIA *is picking up the sack during this; the seam gives
and the grain spills all over the stage. There is total silence.
Everything stops. Everyone looks at the spilled grain.*

ALEXANDRA, *and then the others, including the*
WOMEN *from the valley, go down on their hands and
knees and start gathering the grain, every kernel. They work
in silence.* SOFIA *watches them, and then joins in.*

One of the WOMEN *begins to sob. No one acknowledges
this, and even the sobbing woman doesn't pause in her
work. But* SOFIA *stands slowly, painfully. She lets the
handful of grain she's gathered fall to the ground. She
walks to the sobbing woman, puts her hand on her head.
The woman's crying softens.* SOFIA *leaves. The* WOMEN
*work. We hear the sound of the river, building in volume,
becoming menacing.*

Scene 10

*It is dark night. We hear the sound of the river, louder now
than ever. We see a figure in the darkness, struggling with
something. The figure drags a heavy burden from the river and
then sits heavily, clutching it tightly to her. There is a pause,
the sound of the river and the night. Then someone else enters.
A match is struck;* FIDELIA *is standing, holding the match
and a candle. She lights the candle, approaches the figure on*

the ground. In the candlelight we see SOFIA *sitting, wet, holding a different body.* FIDELIA *kneels beside her. She blows out the candle. They sit in the dark.*

Scene 11

Headlights of a jeep sweeping first the auditorium, then the stage as though the vehicle was rounding a hill and coming to a stop. The headlights catch SOFIA, *clutching the body.* FIDELIA *stands, backs away.*

LIEUTENANT (*offstage*). There! There! It's . . . Who the fuck . . . Who the fuck is . . . (*Giving orders.*) Go around that side, that side, cover the right, GO! (*He enters, behind him soldiers,* SOFIA *clutches the body tighter.*)

Nobody move, nobody move! Get away from that . . .

ALEXANDRA *enters from the other side.*

ALEXANDRA. Fidelia! Fidelia! Come here, come here, quickly . . . Sofia.

A second set of headlights pulls in from the opposite direction, tyres on gravel coming to a halt. The CAPTAIN *enters, behind him* EMMANUEL.

CAPTAIN. What the . . . What is going on here, what is . . .

LIEUTENANT. Get away from that, you old cunt.

CAPTAIN. What's she got, Mrs. Fuentes, what are you . . . Oh my God.

LIEUTENANT. I said get away from that you disgusting old cunt.

He takes his gun out of his holster.

CAPTAIN. Lieutenant. Lieutenant. Put that away.

The LIEUTENANT *doesn't seem to hear the* CAPTAIN. *He cocks the gun.* ALEXANDRA *steps in between the* LIEUTENANT *and* SOFIA. *Other* WOMEN *enter, stand at a distance watching.*

YANINA. Don't shoot her, don't.

ALEXANDRA. She's just an old woman, there are witnesses, don't . . .

CAPTAIN. Lieutenant, put the gun down and get back in the jeep.

The CAPTAIN *pushes* ALEXANDRA *aside and stands between the lieutenant and the old woman.*

I am giving you an order. Get back in the jeep.

The LIEUTENANT *hesitates, lowers his gun, turns and leaves.*

(*To the* WOMEN.) Go home. There's nothing here. Go home.

No one moves. He turns to the old woman.

Mrs. Fuentes. Mrs. Fuentes. Get away from the body.

Where did you . . . Did you find it in the . . . Mrs. Fuentes?

Mrs. Fuentes, will you put that down so we can take a look and see if . . .

SOFIA (*not looking up*). Alexandra?

ALEXANDRA. What, Sofia?

SOFIA. Miguel . . .

CAPTAIN. What did she . . .

ALEXANDRA. She said . . . She thinks it's her husband. She thinks . . .

SOFIA. Miguel.

Pause.

CAPTAIN (*to* ALEXANDRA). Listen. We'll take the body and . . .

SOFIA. NO.

CAPTAIN. I will personally take responsibility for this body. There will be an official . . . We are as concerned about this as . . .

SOFIA. You. Listen to me.

> You will have to kill me. Do you understand. You'll have to kill me first.

CAPTAIN (*looks around him at the* WOMEN). I understand.

> Do you . . . Do you want help . . .

SOFIA. No help.

ALEXANDRA. We'll carry him. Sofia. Sofia, come.

> *The other* WOMEN *approach. Together they all pick up the body, heavy with river water. They carry it past the soldiers and out.*

CAPTAIN. TWO fucking bodies! TWO! Someone is setting me up, I . . .

> Tell the Lieutenant to get his butt over here. Now.

EMMANUEL *exits.*

CAPTAIN. Stink-hole. Fucking stink-hole. Plug the god-damned river up. Make a . . . a lake. With a concrete bottom. Clean. Paddle-boats on Sundays. That's better. That's it.

> *The* LIEUTENANT *enters,* EMMANUEL *behind. The* LIEUTENANT *and the* CAPTAIN *glare at each other. The* CAPTAIN *makes* EMMANUEL *leave.*

LIEUTENANT. Where do you think these bodies are coming from?

CAPTAIN. Where do you think they're coming from?

LIEUTENANT. I asked you first.

CAPTAIN. I'm your superior.

LIEUTENANT. Then you must be smarter than me.

CAPTAIN. I am.

LIEUTENANT. Then answer my question. Sir.

CAPTAIN. I think someone wants to make trouble for me.

LIEUTENANT. I think someone wants to make trouble for me.

CAPTAIN. Who? Why would anyone want to do that? You're such a charming young man.

LIEUTENANT. But some people, I think, are immune to my charms.

The Communists. The Terrorists. The Subversives. That old woman. She's doing it! They're tossing these bodies in, using you to get rid of people like me, people who are effective. If Fuentes is buried, then she'll ask who killed him, and then they ask who arrested him, and then they trace a trail back to me.

CAPTAIN. Paranoid bullshit. You're doing it! You and your effective friends! You throw the bodies in the river so she can find them and she gets wild and I am expected to abandon my programme and start shooting . . .

LIEUTENANT. Oh, shooting! You're so delicate, captain. This, this reform, this delicacy, it will end with me on trial. And you on trial too, for what you did somewhere else, can't you see that?

CAPTAIN. There'll be no trials. Trials come when bodies float downstream. So in case you happen to know who's throwing them in . . .

LIEUTENANT. I DON'T KNOW WHO . . .

CAPTAIN (*overlapping*). Tell them to be smart, ask themselves what their best interests really are, because at this moment-- it's in my best interest to point my guns not at these women but at . . . anyone I see getting in my way.

Little pause.

LIEUTENANT. I thank you for your friendly, middle-class advice. And here's some for you.

Everything we do here is being watched. By important people. The true defenders of the motherland . . . So if the funeral happens, an hour later you'll get a phone call announcing your demotion. And a day or two later you'll find yourself back in the capital where the streets are crowded and cars speed by and one speeding past you some morning has a man inside with a gun and a bullet.

CAPTAIN. Save your threats, you . . .

LIEUTENANT. And back here in the valley of hell the guns will be pointed at our enemies again. You betrayed me. You sided with that crow. All of those women saw that.

CAPTAIN. Lieutenant . . .

LIEUTENANT. I mean it, Captain. Don't let her bury that body.

The LIEUTENANT *nods, leaves.*

On another side of the stage, the Fuentes family enters with the body. Silently washes it and prepares it for burial.

CAPTAIN (*apparently alone*). Damn.

You were listening the whole time?

Emmanuel?

EMMANUEL *appears.*

CAPTAIN. My little shadow. I wish you wouldn't do that.

I think . . . I may have gone too far.

EMMANUEL. The Lieutenant seemed upset.

CAPTAIN. How observant.

EMMANUEL. May I make a suggestion? Captain?

CAPTAIN. Oh please do. You're so thoroughly informed, after all.

EMMANUEL. You didn't know Miguel Fuentes. Maybe you made a mistake.

CAPTAIN. A mistake.

EMMANUEL. If someone else claimed the body, a competing claim. Maybe it was someone else's husband. Someone whose husband died accidentally. There are men missing the Lieutenant didn't arrest, whose funerals wouldn't worry the Lieutenant.

CAPTAIN. Got anyone in mind?

EMMANUEL. Theo Sanjines.

CAPTAIN. Someone you . . .

EMMANUEL. I know his wife. . . Cecilia Sanjines. My
girlfriend. Now she is.

CAPTAIN. Urqueta was right. You're a credit to your kind.

You eavesdrop on my conversations. You probably open my
mail. Whose ears are you? Who do you listen for? Kastoria?

Little pause.

EMMANUEL. With your permission, Captain, but I want to
leave this place. So does Cecilia. And Felipe Kastoria
doesn't seem to think that's such a good idea.

CAPTAIN. Does Kastoria know about the bodies?

EMMANUEL. Mr. Kastoria used to say, sir: 'Not a leaf falls
on my land without me knowing it.'

CAPTAIN. The Kastorias must be close to the Lieutenant. The
Families.

EMMANUEL. There are luncheons, sir, the Lieutenant is
invited.

CAPTAIN. Uh huh.

If you happen to find yourself upriver again, it would be in
your interests to give Mr. Kastoria the impression . . . that
I am in control. Because, Orderly, if I succeed here I will be
very grateful to those who help me.

Now. I think our co-operative widow. . .

EMMANUEL. Mrs. Sanjines.

CAPTAIN. Should be informed that her husband has drowned.
A most unpleasant task. I'm sure you'll find a way of
comforting her.

EMMANUEL. Yes sir. . . And what about . . . the old woman,
sir?

CAPTAIN (*he sits at the river bank in* SOFIA'*s spot*). If I sit
like her, will a body come to me?

Where, where where are the bodies coming from?

Little pause.

That old woman's grandson. How old?

EMMANUEL. Um, thirteen, fourteen, I . . .

CAPTAIN (*standing*). A little detour through the shit. To the future. God willing.

Scene 12

CECILIA *and* EMMANUEL.

EMMANUEL. You want him to come back.

CECILIA. I want you.

EMMANUEL. Then bury him.

CECILIA. But that's not him.

EMMANUEL. It is if you say so.

CECILIA. No. It's someone else. Theo will come back . . .

EMMANUEL. Bury him and he won't.

CECILIA. I wish it was that simple.

EMMANUEL. It is. Listen to me: Bury him and he'll never come back. You do this for the Captain and the Captain will make certain Theo never shows up again.

Little pause.

CECILIA. I can't do that.

EMMANUEL. Choose. Him or me.

Little pause, then CECILIA *kisses* EMMANUEL.

CECILIA. Promise me: When we get to the city we'll have thousands of children.

EMMANUEL. Millions, not thousands, millions.

CECILIA. And every one of them with your eyes.

Scene 13

The Fuentes family gathered in a room around the body,
washed and dressed now and laid out on a rough bier. Red
sunrise, candles.

SOFIA. When I was just a girl, my sisters and I went to town,
dressed in bright dresses our grandma made, for the festival
of the planting. You could see the torches in the square from
afar off, all the way up the mountain, and we rode down in
a cart . . . It was so late when we got to the square, and my
sisters, may they rest in peace, they vanished right away,
into the crowd, all those tall farmers . . . and there was
music and then I felt his hands on my shoulders, behind me.
He said don't turn around, and he took my red scarf and
covered my eyes, and tied it behind me, so all I could see
when I opened my eyes was bright red. And he led me blind
to the dance.

FIDELIA. Then what?

SOFIA. I've told you so often what happened next. We danced.
I couldn't see him. I felt him. He was only a boy, but I was
only a girl, and the band started playing something, a song
with a strange rhythm I didn't know, and I said to him take
off this scarf, you idiot, I can't see and I don't know how to
do this dance, and he said leave it on I'll teach you, and I
said why should you see when I can't? And he said he
couldn't see either, his eyes were closed. And I thought that
was funny so I let him dance with me even though I thought
probably he's crazy. Miguel. And after the dance was over
he took off the scarf and looked at me and said Oh! You're
beautiful.

FIDELIA. Were you?

SOFIA. No, I was ugly. But that's what he said.

I could always recognise him, from that night on, even with
my eyes closed, even blind, in the dark. I could always
recognise my Miguel.

Scene 14

FATHER GABRIEL *and the* CAPTAIN.

CAPTAIN. I'm troubled. You've heard about the body in the river. It can't be properly identified. But a widow claims it as the body of her man. So I've taken a risk. It seemed, well . . .

FATHER GABRIEL. Compassionate.

CAPTAIN. Yes. To let her have the body to bury.

Have I sinned in allowing her this funeral, even though I have my doubts that the corpse is hers?

FATHER GABRIEL. I've asked myself the same question, Captain.

CAPTAIN. Yes.

FATHER GABRIEL. After all, I have to perform the rites, and . . .

CAPTAIN. Since you aren't certain . . .

FATHER GABRIEL. I've seen the body. I have serious doubts.

CAPTAIN. But?

FATHER GABRIEL. These are troubled times. These women need an end to the uncertainty, the not-knowing is . . . intolerable. It's a peculiar form of Hell. If a burial can bring peace, then in the name of a greater good I would perform the funeral.

CAPTAIN. And trust that the Heavenly Father will forgive.

FATHER GABRIEL. Since we act in the name of peace, yes.

CAPTAIN. I can't tell you how much this relieves me, Father.

FATHER GABRIEL. And it will relieve the torment of Sofia Fuentes.

CAPTAIN. Sofia Fuentes. Ah, then you haven't heard.

That was . . . a mistake. Mrs. Fuentes was mistaken. The body has been claimed by Cecilia Sanjines.

FATHER GABRIEL. Cecilia?

CAPTAIN. Her husband, Theo Sanjines. Missing for seven months. Apparently a heavy drinker, he . . . used to beat his wife. A lot of these men did.

Odd that she hasn't contacted you about the service. No doubt she's still in shock.

Little pause.

FATHER GABRIEL. Captain, I can't . . . You gave that body to Sofia Fuentes.

CAPTAIN. But you yourself said it didn't look like . . .

FATHER GABRIEL. It was unrecognisable. Why is one woman's claim better than another's?

CAPTAIN. In this affair I have had to play Solomon. I can't cut the corpse in two, can I? So the widow whose claim seems most probable gets the body.

Little pause.

FATHER GABRIEL. I won't do it. I can't. Miguel Fuentes was my friend. He sat in the chair you're sitting in, many nights, he . . .

CAPTAIN. Then you'll want to help his family.

FATHER GABRIEL. They won't consider it a help to . . .

CAPTAIN. But they will. You see, in exchange for your pastoral assistance in the funeral of Theo Sanjines, and in exchange for the good-natured co-operation of the Fuentes family, I would be prepared to release a prisoner, a relative of theirs.

FATHER GABRIEL. Emiliano? Alonso?

CAPTAIN. Um, I think his name is Alexis.

FATHER GABRIEL. No, Alexis is the boy.

CAPTAIN. Yes. Him.

Pause.

FATHER GABRIEL. He isn't . . .

CAPTAIN. We arrested him this afternoon.

Little pause.

FATHER GABRIEL. Please. . . please don't hurt the boy.

CAPTAIN. I will tell Mrs. Sanjines to expect your call. Be careful with her, she's very upset.

Hurt the boy?

I know what you think of me, Father.

FATHER GABRIEL. I don't think you do.

CAPTAIN. I can imagine. Don't judge me. I am . . . It sickens me, I hate pain, terror, but at times I'm forced to . . . We have to follow our hearts to the greater good. There are forces at work here – who intend nothing good for this country. I intend peace. I want that as much as you. But sometimes the road to peace is, as you know, fraught with difficult choices. You shouldn't judge me too hastily.

FATHER GABRIEL. I don't, Captain. The dead will judge the dead.

Little pause. The CAPTAIN *kneels.*

CAPTAIN. Bless me Father. For I have sinned.

Lights go down on CAPTAIN *and* FATHER GABRIEL. *Only a light on the chair where the* CAPTAIN *sat remains. From the shadows,* FIDELIA *appears.*

Scene 15

FIDELIA *and the chair.*

FIDELIA. Are you in pain? Are you in pain? Can I do . . . something to help you? Are you in pain?

THE WOMEN (*as lights rise on them*). Yes, he is in pain, yes, Fidelia, he is.

The lights begin to fade on the empty chair and rise on the chair next to it. Seated in this chair is a naked man, breathing heavily, with a black cloth hood over his head. He hardly moves. It is difficult to tell from his body how old he is, but he's very thin.

FIDELIA. What can I do for him, how can I help him, can I go to where he is?

THE WOMEN. No, Fidelia, you can't do that, the door is locked, it's too far.

FIDELIA. Can I give him water, is he thirsty, medicine, is he hurt, what can I . . . ?

THE WOMEN. Talk to him, girl, he can hear you, talk to him, tell him a story.

FIDELIA. A story? A story, I don't . . . What kind of story, a story about what?

THE WOMEN. About this, Fidelia, the story of what happened.

FIDELIA. Not that, that will hurt him, I don't want to tell him that, I can't, I can't . . . .

THE WOMEN. The truth, Fidelia, the story of what happened.

FIDELIA. I don't know how.

I saw a bird, a dead bird, on its back, its throat was pulled back, like this, its beak was open, it was trying to . . . to fly, no, it was . . . trying to drink . . . it was drinking in light, it was trying to do that. No, that's not . . .

The door. They kicked in the door, they splintered, the door. Mama screamed, she screamed . . . about the bird, no, she . . . screamed . . . something, it was . . . 'Take me', she said, I think she . . . but then, but then, but they knew, he was down in the corn, down in the corn, he was hid in the corn but they knew, who told them, and she screamed, and she screamed, but they went through the fields, like fire, so fast, and they trampled the corn, and they picked him, like a plant, they tore at the roots, they picked him out from the corn, and she kept on screaming but making no sounds, and . . .

And where was I, when they took my . . . where was I standing, I was standing by mama, no, I was . . . not, I was out in the corn, I was . . . up in the air I was . . . flying above it and . . . no, I was . . . dead I was . . . lying on my back, trying . . . to drink in the light, but . . . I don't know how to tell you this story, papa, I don't know what story I'm trying to tell, I . . .

Papa? Are you there?

They took him, papa. They took Alexis away.

Scene 16

The cemetery on the hill: generations upon generations of plain peasant graves.

CECILIA, EMMANUEL, *the* CAPTAIN *and the* LIEUTENANT *by a freshly-dug grave. They are waiting for the Fuentes family to deliver the body.* FATHER GABRIEL *stands apart. No one says anything.* ALEXANDRA, YANINA *and* SOFIA *arrive with the corpse.*

ALEXANDRA. Where's my son?

CAPTAIN. Lieutenant, the boy.

The LIEUTENANT *exits. Silence.*

CAPTAIN (*to the* FUENTES WOMEN). I assume you know Mrs. Sanjines.

Silence.

Mrs. Sanjines, you know . . .

CECILIA (*barely audible*). Yes.

Alexandra, I'm sorry.

ALEXANDRA. Theo will kill you.

ALEXANDRA *turns her back on* CECILIA.

CAPTAIN. Ladies, please.

The LIEUTENANT *re-enters with* ALEXIS. *The boy is unsteady on his feet, his shirt has been torn and hastily repatched, he looks at the ground and keeps one eye closed. From the other side of the stage,* FIDELIA *appears with the baby. She watches the scene from afar.*

CAPTAIN (*thrown by the appearance of* ALEXIS). Um . . .
Good. Good . . . now we can . . .

ALEXANDRA *walks to the* LIEUTENANT *and* ALEXIS,
she takes ALEXIS *by the arm, he cries out, pulls away.*
ALEXANDRA *turns to the* CAPTAIN.

ALEXANDRA. What did . . . what did you . . . ?

LIEUTENANT. He's alive. Be thankful. Next time, save us the
trouble.

Captain, your prisoner. (*The* LIEUTENANT *exits.*)

CAPTAIN (*rattled*). Suspected subversives will be interrogated
according to official procedures. Don't misunderstand me.
I am as commited as ever to peace but . . . I cannot permit
subversion of my authority.

Mrs. Fuentes, Thank you for returning the body of Mr.
Sanjines. We apologise for the grotesque mistake. Now take
your grandson and go home.

Mrs. Fuentes.

Mrs. Fuentes.

He goes to ALEXIS, *grabs his arm.* ALEXIS *cries out.*

Woman, you haven't begun to see the trouble I can cause.

ALEXANDRA. Sofia . . .

SOFIA *strengthens her grip on the body. No one moves.
Then she lets go, turns, goes to her grandson, puts an arm
gingerly around him and leads him away from the* CAPTAIN.

The CAPTAIN *signals to the two soldiers. They move to the
cart. They pick up the corpse and carry it to the grave. They
place it in the pit.*

CAPTAIN. Mrs. Sanjines . . .

EMMANUEL *nudges* CECILIA, *who stumbles a little and
then walks quickly to the grave. Not looking in, she pitches
a flower at the corpse and turns and almost exits.*
EMMANUEL *stops her.*

CAPTAIN. Father . . .

FATHER GABRIEL. Father in Heaven, here is . . . one of Your children. We . . .

CAPTAIN. Name.

FATHER GABRIEL. Theo Sanjines. Father, show mercy for my friend Theo Sanjines. Wherever his soul may be.

Ashes to ashes, earth to earth, dust you were and dust you are and to dust you shall return. Amen.

Little pause.

CAPTAIN. Thank you. Mrs. Sanjines, my condolences.

CECILIA *exits quickly.* EMMANUEL *follows her.*

(*To* ALEXANDRA). The army will reimburse you for the cost of the shroud.

Good day.

The CAPTAIN *exits. The two soldiers hastily fill in the grave.*

FATHER GABRIEL. Sofia. God works in strange ways. Maybe this is a sign – that he – that Miguel is alive. You should never give up hope.

Little pause.

Please forgive me. All of you.

Exits.

The soldiers hammer a flimsy wooden cross into the earth at the head of the grave, and exit.

ALEXANDRA. Sofia. Thank you.

SOFIA. Miguel. Is so ashamed of me. (*She exits.*)

ALEXANDRA. Alexis.

ALEXANDRA *goes to* ALEXIS. *She leads him off, followed by* YANINA. FIDELIA *stays behind, always at a distance from the tombs, as if she inhabited a separate dimension. She speaks to the child.*

FIDELIA. Say something. Say 'Ma.' Every baby your age can say 'Ma.' (*She looks at the audience.*)

Maybe he won't ever say anything. Maybe he'll just be quiet.
And never tell a story to anybody. Until the day he dies.

She exits with the baby.

Scene 17

*We watch night fall on the graveyard, and then fade as a dawn
light grows and builds: The graveyard, the next morning, a
beautiful day.* SOFIA *enters, hair unplaited and wild. She is
carrying bread, which she places on Theo's grave. She looks
at the mound. She takes clumps of the earth in her hands and
examines them. She holds it to her face, and inhales deeply.
Then she rubs some of it across her chest, sensually, between
her legs, and then crumbles the remaining earth to the ground.
She picks up the loaf of bread, tears it in half, and puts one
half back on the ground. She is biting into her half when the
first woman enters; she too is carrying bread. Other* WOMEN
*arrive; each, one at a time, tears her loaf in half and leaves
it on Theo's grave, till soon the grave is a mound of freshly-
baked loaves.* YANINA *goes to sit by* SOFIA *at the grave;*
ALEXANDRA *has come too but sits apart. The* WOMEN *sit
around it, eating.*

KATHERINA. I knew when I saw the first body come out of
the river, the minute I laid hands on him I knew it was my
brother. I should have insisted. I was afraid.

TERESA. It wasn't your brother. It was my nephew. I recognised him. I was too afraid to speak. When you said to the
lieutenant that you thought you recognised your brother,
I thought to myself, she's crazy, she's wrong but at least
she has the courage to speak.

ROSA. The first body, well I can't be absolutely certain but the
hands, even broken, I think it was Luisa's oldest son. I am
absolutely sure that the second body, though, was . . .

TERESA. That was my husband. No doubt about that.

MARILUZ. My father.

ROSA. My father. I baked all night. This is my father in this grave. I baked bread for his grave.

TERESA. This is very confusing.

AMANDA. Everyone baked. All night. The whole valley smelled of yeast rising.

TERESA. So does everyone think . . . ?

KATHERINA. Maybe it isn't anyone's. Maybe everyone's wrong.

MARILUZ. Maybe everyone's right.

TERESA. Impossible. It can't belong to all of us. It's only one body.

KATHERINA. Yes. And it's my son, Eduardo.

TERESA. It's Antonio. It's my husband. He was that thin.

ROSA. It's my father.

MARILUZ. No, mine. Ernesto Torres. I'd stake my life on it.

AMANDA. It didn't look a thing like your father, he wasn't nearly so tall, it was . . .

LUCIA. It was Cesar. That pig. He beat me, I hated him, I was going to leave the bastard, but then they took him. As long as I didn't know if he was alive or dead I was stuck with him forever. Now I can . . .

TERESA. You can what?

LUCIA. Dig up the little shit, bury him proper, and then dance on his grave.

Some of the WOMEN *laugh,* KATHERINA *hushes them.*

TERESA. But it's only one body. And everyone wants to bury it.

What are we going to do about that?

SOFIA. You know what to do. You told me how to do it.

Go get permission. And then bury your men.

TERESA. But it's just this one poor . . .

SOFIA. That's not our problem. You identify? Then you must bury. Ask permission. Let the captain figure it out.

The WOMEN *start to stand. The cry of a bird, overhead. Then the lights begin to change. There is the sound of the river, and a sense of rushing water, and something magical. One of the* WOMEN *speaks first, and the others join in under her, perhaps singing, or chanting, or repeating her incantation.*

THE WOMEN. The water knows, the water has been there, the water is curious, it wants to find out, it will flood in your ears, in your eyes, in your mouth it will carry out the words, from the deepest places, the memories the pain, it will carry your stories over miles of river, calling the stories as it moves to the sea, it will sing to the valleys with a stony voice, the water the throat drinks, the rain that he sees the mud that he walks in the soup that they eat the sweat that falls and the other water the other water and some rivers are wide, and calm, green and smooth, and some are sharp and high, they fall clear from the mountains, and ours is a river that is shallow, cold and brown, and it brings us our men, over miles of stone beds, it tumbles them home, but there are so many men who are missing or dead, so many the river cannot carry them all, too many stories for the river to tell too many stories so it brought us back one, and the godless they burnt it, and it brought us another, to bury on the hill, and it tumbled the body, over and over, till all of its features were murmured away . . . because if the river carried all the men home, their bodies would dam it, they would strangle the river, and the valley would flood, and the field turn to swamp, where nothing can grow, and everything rots, and it found us this body, and it made it any body, and it made it every body, and it's mine, it's mine, oh please don't let it be mine, it's mine, oh please don't let it be mine, it's mine, oh please, oh please, oh please, oh please . . .

The WOMEN *then each in turn individually say: 'It's mine.'*

End of Act II.

ACT III

Scene 18

The CAPTAIN *and* EMMANUEL; *the widows queued up.*
TERESA SALAS *in a chair.*

CAPTAIN. Thirty-six widows! What the fuck am I supposed
to do with thirty-six widows! Widows, mothers, aunts,
grandmas – the only woman in the whole miserable fucking
valley who isn't demanding that corpse is the one woman
we gave it to! And where the fuck is she, Orderly?

EMMANUEL. I can't find her, Captain, I don't know . . .

CAPTAIN. You seem to know a whole fuck of a lot less than I
thought you did, this whole mess, well, I'd say it was all
your fault if you were important enough to matter, but you
don't, you're just my little peasant orderly who tries too
hard to be helpful and I let myself forget, no progress
without order, but now I'm taking control.

Your girlfriend's the official widow in this hideous mess and
if you want me to transfer you out of here you'd better find
her.

EMMANUEL *salutes and exits.*

CAPTAIN. Someone's set me up, someone's making a joke of
me, the press will hear about this and then . . . We don't do
well in sports or beauty contests. Finally we have a record
to be proud of: more widows per corpse than any other
country in the world.

TERESA. My name is Teresa Salas, I am 53 years old, my
husband Antonio Salas, he would have been 59 years old
last March, he was mayor of Camacho. He was elected
when we last had an election; when we stopped having
elections, he was arrested for trying to reclaim the land.
And taken away on February 20th eight years ago and
I never saw him again. Until two days ago when . . . when

his body washed up in the river. And now I want to bury him. In the cemetery by his parents' graves.

CAPTAIN (*flipping through a stack of claims*). Husband brother husband father son nephew son son . . . lover . . . husband husband uncle husband . . .

So which woman's claim is . . .

I mean it can't belong to all of you. It's only one body.

TERESA. My husband's.

CAPTAIN. So the other women are wrong.

Pause.

Right? One of you is right and the other thirty-six have to be mistaken. Right?

TERESA. It's not my job to explain. I know what I know. They know what they know. I know it is my husband.

CAPTAIN. You don't know you don't know that's the point, none of you knows. anything, you're all mentally underdeveloped emotionally overdeveloped superstitious mindless peasants and this . . . preposterous little scandal you've cooked up – you have no idea the trouble this is causing, you have no idea . . . what you're spoiling here with this demented, backwards . . .

TERESA (*pulling a locket from her blouse, moving with startling energy and abruptness to the* CAPTAIN, *speaking vehemently*). Backwards? Is it backwards to want to bury your dead? Don't you want your wife to do it for you? This is my husband who I lived with for thirty-two years – no, don't look away.

She tears the locket from her neck, slams it on the desk.

This is my husband I slept with every night for thirty-two years, what do you mean how do I know? What do you mean backwards? I know.

CAPTAIN (*quietly, picking up the locket*). Enough, Mrs. Salas.

TERESA. They shot my sixteen year old son in the back of his head. I . . . saw . . . that. They . . . did . . . that.

CAPTAIN (*still quiet*). I said that's enough.

TERESA. If this is not my husband, then where is he? If this is not his body, then give him to me alive. If you won't do that, then let me bury him.

Pause.

CAPTAIN. You want to bury this body that you say is your husband.

But what if your husband . . . walked through that door now?

What if I clap my hands, like this: (*He claps.*) and he walked through the door.

The door begins to open; TERESA spins around towards it. The LIEUTENANT enters. TERESA stares at him then looks away.

What would you do if your husband came through that door?

TERESA. I would thank you, Captain. If he came back alive. What else could I do?

CAPTAIN. Yes.

That's all, Mrs. Salas.

I said that's all.

Tell the next widow I'm going to lunch.

She exits.

I didn't call for you.

LIEUTENANT. I wanted to gloat.

CAPTAIN. Gloat somewhere else. I'm busy. There are seventeen other . . .

LIEUTENANT. This is more fun than a circus. The Captain and his amazing multiplying widows. What's your next trick?

CAPTAIN. A surprise.

LIEUTENANT. Take control here. That'd surprise everyone.

CAPTAIN. I'll tell you a story.

My father had a dog, and he beat it every day.

LIEUTENANT. Captain, I really don't want to . . .

CAPTAIN. Sit down and shut the fuck up and listen to my story, Lieutenant. That's an order.

My father had this dog . . .

LIEUTENANT. And he beat it every day.

CAPTAIN. Right. Then one day, without warning, it bit him. Locked onto him. I was alone with him in the house. He sent me for his pistol – he was a Colonel – he told me how to load it, all this. with the dog eating up his arm, screaming at me, my father – and when it was loaded, I shot the dog. And it still wouldn't let go. It had finally gotten what it wanted after all those years of beatings and even after death it wasn't going to let go. So I had to get his hunting knife and begin to work on its teeth. I was seven years old.

LIEUTENANT. That's . . . illuminating. A parable. You shot the dog.

CAPTAIN. Had to.

LIEUTENANT. Will you shoot here?

CAPTAIN. Ah, but you miss the parable's point. You're too easily distracted by guns.

LIEUTENANT. So what's the point?

CAPTAIN. The point is: When you back people against the wall, they may surrender. Or they may put up a fight that will leave you crippled. My father was never able to use that arm again in his life.

People get hurt. That's the point.

LIEUTENANT. These people are used to being beaten. The point here is: make sure they don't forget who's holding the leash. If you are holding the leash.

At least you've got me to command. You're my captain, Captain. Bow wow.

CAPTAIN. I'll tell you something: There's a part of me that would love to shoot one or two of those women. There's a part of me that would love to shoot you.

But any thug can use a gun. They can make trouble and you can make threats, but we have to move ahead, and we'll drag the rest of you kicking and screaming into the twentieth century.

LIEUTENANT. The twentieth century? We're already there.

CAPTAIN. Not in this country we're not.

LIEUTENANT. On the contrary. What would the twentieth century be without countries like ours?

So what bone will you throw them?

CAPTAIN. Now that's the real surprise.

Scene 19

EMMANUEL *and* CECILIA *at the river; she's got a suitcase and she's dishevelled, clambering along the riverbank with* EMMANUEL *in pursuit.*

EMMANUEL. You're fucking everything up, please, baby, you have to . . .

CECILIA. I have to get away from here. You lied. You said he wasn't coming back, but he is, he'll see the grave, they'll tell him what I . . .

EMMANUEL. He's dead. Theo is dead.

CECILIA. He's not.

EMMANUEL. I killed him.

CECILIA. You're a liar.

EMMANUEL. You don't want him dead. You don't love me.

CECILIA. Take me to the city. Now. Then I'll be better. Then I can forget, I can't here, but there . . . We have to go now, we . . .

She stops suddenly, looking ahead of her at the river.

CECILIA. Oh no, oh no . . .

EMMANUEL. What? What is it? Celia?

In a terrible panic CECILIA *begins running away from the river. He stands, pulling his gun out, looking where she's looked. He sees nothing, he runs after her, grabs her.*

CECILIA (*wild with terror*). Let me go, let me . . .

EMMANUEL. What's wrong what's wrong, there's nothing . . .

CECILIA. It's him! It's him! In the river, it's . . .

EMMANUEL. There's nothing in the river!

CECILIA. Theo's in the water, I saw . . .

She breaks away and now begins to run towards the river.

EMMANUEL. Stop, Cecilia, goddamn it I said stop! (*He fires his gun into the air. She stops but doesn't turn to look at him.*)

CECILIA. Don't. Please don't kill me.

EMMANUEL *walks past her to the river.*

CECILIA. Oh God forgive me, God forgive me . . .

EMMANUEL. Shut up, shut the fuck up. It's . . .

EMMANUEL *wades into the river. He returns carrying a wet tattered piece of black cloth.*

EMMANUEL. See? Nothing. River trash. See.

Scared the shit out of me. Women . . .

See?

CECILIA. Put the gun away.

EMMANUEL (*putting the gun away*). Did you really think it was . . .

CECILIA. It was. I thought it was. Yes.

EMMANUEL. But it wasn't.

They stand looking at each other, winded.

EMMANUEL. It wasn't. Say it wasn't Theo.

CECILIA. It . . . wasn't him.

EMMANUEL. Say 'Theo's never coming back.' (*Pause.*) Say 'Theo's never coming back.' (*Pause.*) I'm leaving.

He starts to exit, she follows, he turns.

EMMANUEL. You stay. By the river. With him.

Just don't . . . Don't come near me again.

CECILIA. I can't be alone. I'll kill myself.

EMMANUEL. I'm going to the city. That's where I belong. I'll find a woman there without dirty hands, a woman who's never washed in a river. Peasant.

CECILIA. I'll kill myself.

EMMANUEL. I hope you all do. It's deep enough here. Do it.

Scene 20

The CAPTAIN *alone on stage. As he speaks the* WOMEN *of the village assemble, except* FIDELIA, *who watches from the other side of the stage with the baby in her arms. Next to her is* ALEXIS.

CAPTAIN. When I arrived here in Camacho I believed . . . we had a bargain. That I would exercise my authority with reason and restraint, and you would learn to look forward to what life could become.

Well I've lived up to my side of the bargain and you haven't lived up to yours.

You have made yourselves a spectacle, with this half-witted conspiracy to mock me, but . . . We are stuck with one another. And I intend to show you that you can forgive your adversaries and even do them a service. In the name of that future life.

I am pleased to release the first prisoner under the terms of the amnesty decree.

You see, whoever it is dumping dead bodies in the river can only give you dead bodies. I can give you living men.

He claps his hands. There is an absolute silence – none of the WOMEN *is breathing. Two soldiers come in escorting a man, who walks stooped and stiff. They lead him to face the woman. He never raises his head.*

There is another silence. None of the WOMEN *move. They stare at the man - maybe they recognise him, or are afraid they do.*

CAPTAIN (*clearing his throat*). Sofia Fuentes. This afternoon. Alonso Fuentes. Your son.

Scene 21

Lights change and everyone leaves, except the Fuentes WOMEN *as the Fuentes' house materialises around them.* YANINA *takes the baby from* FIDELIA.

YANINA. He's coming back, my heavy little man, I promised you he would. He's tall, your papa, like a tree, but don't be scared of him.

ALEXANDRA. We have to hurry, he'll be here soon.

ALEXANDRA *takes the baby from* YANINA *and gives him to* ALEXIS, *who leaves as* SOFIA *enters with the bathing equipment.* YANINA *removes her widow's black. She's naked, although partially hidden from the audience by the* WOMEN *who surround her and bathe her.*

SOFIA. Don't catch cold.

When they're done, SOFIA *takes a blanket and wraps* YANINA *in it. They exit.* ALEXANDRA *and* FIDELIA *are left alone in the yard.*

FIDELIA. Why did they let Alonso go, and not papa?

Pause.

Are you happy for Yani, mama?

ALEXANDRA (*smiling a little*). Oh Fidelia. Why do you always ask such . . . hard questions? Come here.

Mother and daughter stand looking at each other.

ALEXANDRA. Your father too. He asks hard questions. You're both pains in the ass.

When the women were claiming they recognised . . . For a moment I almost wanted it to be him, it would almost be a relief. Do you understand?

FIDELIA. Yes, mama.

ALEXANDRA. You're a smart girl.

I can't tell you how much I hurt.

YANINA *appears in the doorway in a brilliant green dress.* ALEXANDRA *turns around.*

ALEXANDRA (*after a little pause*). Where? Where did you . . .

YANINA. Alonso. When I got pregnant he went into town and bought it for me. He said so he'd remember, when I got big with the baby, what I'd look like after the baby was born. I never wore it, since he . . . went away before. Do . . . Do I look OK?

ALEXANDRA. You look . . . you look like a fancy lady.

YANINA. How fancy?

ALEXANDRA. Ten pesos an hour.

They look at each other and both start to laugh.

YANINA. Oh Alex. Oh Alex I'm so sorry . . .

ALEXANDRA. Shut up.

YANINA. Do I smell okay?

ALEXANDRA. Mmmm. Like pine sap. Mmmm.

YANINA. Like on my wedding night.

ALEXANDRA. On your wedding night you smelled like cheap wine.

ALEXIS *comes into the yard from the house carrying the baby.*

YANINA. Oh I got so drunk . . .

They laugh and embrace. ALONSO *steps into the yard. The*
WOMEN *don't see him.* ALEXIS *does. He looks at*
ALONSO *for a moment and then says:.*

ALEXIS. Ma . . . ? Mama, he's . . .

YANINA and ALEXANDRA *turn. A frozen moment, then*
YANINA *runs to* ALONSO *and they embrace.* SOFIA *and*
FIDELIA *come out of the house.*

SOFIA. We've made some soup, it will . . .

SOFIA *and* ALONSO *look at each other. Behind him, the*
other WOMEN *of the valley drift in.*

YANINA. Sofia? Sofia come here, it's your son, don't you . . .

Look how thin he is, he's so thin, and pale you can see
through him almost, Sofia.

SOFIA. It's not him.

YANINA. What are you talking about, of course it is, it's . . .

SOFIA. It's his body but it's not him.

YANINA. Oh she's lost her mind completely, Alexandra, tell
her to . . .

SOFIA. Where's his soul? What have they done with his soul?
Ask him that.

His soul's with the others. Ask him where they are.

Ask him what he did . . . to make them let his body go?

What did you do, my baby? Who did you have to betray?

YANINA. Oh God she . . . Sofia, stop. This is Alonso, this is
your son, he . . .

He never had anything to do with that, with politics, what
could he have done, betray, he didn't know anything,
Alonso, tell her, tell her you don't know what she's talking
about, tell her . . .

She goes to ALEXIS, *takes the baby from him.*

Look, this is your son, this is . . .

ALONSO. I . . . Yes. I . . .

YANINA. Come inside, come inside, don't you want to . . .

ALONSO *kneels slowly. He lowers his head.*

ALONSO. They keep you blindfolded in a room. You know where they're taking you by how many steps. Thirty-one steps is the bathroom. Forty-four is exercise. If you go over sixty steps and down a staircase there's no other place they can be taking you. Every day. And they said 'Just one name and . . . So I . . . And they wanted more names, so I . . . Every name I knew.

(*To* YANINA.) Your name.

YANINA (*fierce*). Whatever you had to do to live. I don't care. Whatever he had to do.

ALEXANDRA. Is . . . Where's Emiliano? Do you . . .

ALONSO *stands. He turns in a full circle, looking at all the* WOMEN *around him.*

ALONSO. I haven't seen him. I haven't seen anyone. Since the day they took us. They split us up and I haven't seen anyone since. They split us up and I haven't seen him since.

SOFIA *goes to him, takes his hand, kisses it, and sings very softly, a lullaby without words. When she's done she lets go his hand and turns away.*

SOFIA. Yani. Alonso's tired. Feed him. Put him to bed.

SOFIA *goes into the house. We see the empty chair illuminated. She goes to it.*

YANINA (*to all the* WOMEN). Whatever he had to do.

SOFIA *returns with Emiliano's chair.*

ALEXANDRA. That's Emiliano's chair. Where are you going with my husband's chair?

SOFIA. To the river.

ALEXANDRA. Why?

SOFIA. You know why.

Poor Alexandra. So good and strong.

They send me back my men. The first two by the river, the third by the road. All dead. Now I go back to the river. To wait for the last.

Scene 22

SOFIA *at the river with the chair.* TERESA *enters, dragging a chair behind her.*

SOFIA. What are you doing here?

TERESA. I came to wait too.

SOFIA. Whose chair?

TERESA. My brother's.

SOFIA. Sebastian?

TERESA. No. Fernando.

SOFIA. It's bitter tonight. You'll catch cold.

TERESA. I'm just as tough as you.

SOFIA. Start a fire. We're both old.

TERESA. There's no wood.

They look at the chairs. TERESA *sets hers on fire. Then* SOFIA *does.*

Good fire. It makes me angry.

SOFIA. Two chairs. It's not much heat.

TERESA. Not yet. There'll be others.

Scene 23

EMMANUEL *at the Kastorias. We see two huge leather armchairs, facing upstage, cigar smoke curling up from them;*

they're both occupied but we can't see their occupants at first:
PHILIP KASTORIA *and his* BROTHER. *We will see Philip
where indicated but we never see the brother. The brother
speaks with a flat, slightly mechanical, very gravelly voice.*
EMMANUEL *stands diffidently by* BEATRICE. PHILIP
stands off to one side, staring out a window.

PHILIP KASTORIA. Tell your captain I am not reassured.

EMMANUEL. Yes, Mr. Kastoria.

PHILIP KASTORIA. Two bodies, and now this multitude of
widows.

I mean how much longer is this going to go on?

And this business of letting politicals go. I mean what is
that? Whose idea of restoring order is that?

You're sure we can't get you something to drink, Emmanuel?

EMMANUEL. No, thank you very much, Mr. Kastoria.

BEATRICE KASTORIA. Are they feeding you, Emmanuel?
You look thin.

PHILIP KASTORIA. Boy's always been thin, Beatrice.

BEATRICE KASTORIA. I've never forgiven Mr. Kastoria for
giving you over to the army.

EMMANUEL. Thank you, Mrs. Kastoria.

BEATRICE KASTORIA. The people we have now are strange
to us. I don't like them. Why don't you come back?

PHILIP KASTORIA. He's useful to me. The others are
dribbling idiots.

EMMANUEL. Thank you, Mr. Kastoria.

PHILIP KASTORIA (*standing up, moving from chair*). I think
your Captain is making a royal mess of this. My brother
agrees. (*Gestures to the chair.*)

I'd like you to tell your Captain that.

EMMANUEL. I think, Mr. Kastoria, that he's only trying to ...

KASTORIA'S BROTHER. Lax.

EMMANUEL (*didn't catch it*). Excuse me, please, I'm sorry
but I ...

KASTORIA'S BROTHER. Philip, tell him to tell his Captain
that he's being lax. Eight years of hard work will come
undone overnight, before you know it they'll be climbing
the fence, like before, digging their twisted fingers into our
land again. Kill a few more if they haven't learned the
lesson yet. God help us when the lower echelon military
starts to think. Squeamish? Replace him. Demote him. Give
his job to this boy here. Someone who'll cut it dead. This
has been going on for weeks. End it. Tell him that, Philip.

PHILIP KASTORIA. Yes, well . . .

KASTORIA'S BROTHER. What, the foreign press? Buried on
page fifty of the afternoon edition. They don't want to read
this garbage. They want to read about a little American girl
trapped in a well. In . . . *Texas!*

He laughs, enjoying saying 'Texas'.

Texas!

BEATRICE KASTORIA. I admire the Captain.

KASTORIA'S BROTHER. Philip, she's starting again . . .

BEATRICE KASTORIA. What do they want, these women?
The bodies of their husbands?

PHILIP KASTORIA. Beatrice please.

BEATRICE KASTORIA. Well give them what they ask for,
it's the Christian thing.

PHILIP KASTORIA. Mrs. Kastoria has been nervous,
Emmanuel, she . . .

BEATRICE KASTORIA. Why do you always say I'm nervous
when I disagree with you? I'm not nervous. I'm afraid.

You know what I overheard the cooks in the kitchen saying,
Emmanuel?

PHILIP KASTORIA. Oh not this . . .

BEATRICE KASTORIA. They were talking about the women
at the river, and they were saying that they'd heard that
bodies were turning up everywhere, even here, even on our
property, in the private fields, in the orchards.

PHILIP KASTORIA (*making a ghost sound*). Oooooooooo . . .

BEATRICE KASTORIA. Shut up, Philip.

They were whispering but I could hear them. They said . . . that these corpses, they were decomposing and faceless. . .

PHILIP KASTORIA. Beatrice, please, that's very unpleasant.

BEATRICE KASTORIA. . . . and at night . . . they said they'd seen them walking around, dirty, and nothing could stop them because nothing can stop the dead.

KASTORIA'S BROTHER *laughs*.

BEATRICE KASTORIA. That's what she said, 'Nothing can stop the dead.' And two nights ago, Philip I didn't tell you this but I woke up from a bad dream and I went downstairs and . . . and they'd left all the doors and windows open. The servants. Had left everything open. So that the dead could come in.

PHILIP KASTORIA (*going to her*). Bea, Bea . . .

You see, Emmanuel, why women wouldn't make good soldiers.

This is why this situation has to come to an end. It's gotten to be intolerable. I want you to tell your commanding officer that.

EMMANUEL. I will sir.

PHILIP KASTORIA. Or I'll have to use my own men. Understand?

EMMANUEL. Yes sir. I understand. I'll make sure the Captain understands.

The LIEUTENANT *enters.*

LIEUTENANT. Oh I think the captain is starting to understand all sorts of things, Emmanuel.

KASTORIA'S BROTHER. Ah, our saviour. I was on the phone to your father this morning.

In the background we see the other WOMEN *join* SOFIA *and the first woman at the riverbank. They carry wooden chairs.*

BEATRICE KASTORIA. Look, Philip, in the valley. Smoke.

LIEUTENANT. Yes, the women. All thirty-six widows. Building a bonfire.

Actually one isn't there. She drowned herself this morning. (*To* EMMANUEL.) I think it was someone you know.

EMMANUEL *spins around to face the* LIEUTENANT. *They stare at each other.*

PHILIP KASTORIA (*looking at the smoke*). What in hell is going on?

LIEUTENANT. The whole village. Burning chairs.

KASTORIA'S BROTHER. Once they get their hands on fire . . .

PHILIP KASTORIA. That does it. I'm taking this into my own hands.

LIEUTENANT. That won't be necessary. I know this Captain. All he needed was time.

Scene 24

The CAPTAIN *and the* LIEUTENANT *in the* CAPTAIN's *office.*

LIEUTENANT. It's an impressive blaze. It can be seen for miles. Everyone who sees it will wonder: who is in command in Camacho?

Little pause.

CAPTAIN. What do they want? I gave them back a. . . I showed them. How to get some of their men back, but they. . . it's like they're in love with death, begging me to pull the trigger.

LIEUTENANT. They want all their men back. Not just one. Not just some. All.

CAPTAIN. All? That's impossible.

LIEUTENANT. Impossible.

No more.

CAPTAIN. What?

LIEUTENANT. No more. That's all they'll say.

CAPTAIN. No more what?

LIEUTENANT. Ask them. No more.

CAPTAIN. You must be very pleased.

LIEUTENANT. Pleased?

CAPTAIN. Well, you were right. Now you'll get what you want. My resignation. And targets. Maybe hundreds. Vindication, recreation.

LIEUTENANT. Recreation? Captain, that's unfair. You think I enjoy this? That boy the other day? You think I enjoyed that?

CAPTAIN. Did you?

LIEUTENANT. I have a brother his age. You've tried to make things better for them, and predictably they'll have to suffer for your good intentions.

They get the butt-end of everything, these people. I pity them.

CAPTAIN. And you despise me.

LIEUTENANT. Captain. We are wearing the same uniform.

CAPTAIN. Meaning you are ready to step into my boots.

LIEUTENANT. Meaning we share the same mother. Meaning that, like brothers, we stand by each other when mistakes are made.

Little pause.

I am yours to command.

Little pause.

CAPTAIN. Perhaps. . . perhaps I have. . . misjudged you.

Little pause.

Arrest the old Fuentes woman.

LIEUTENANT. I suggest a more direct approach.

CAPTAIN. Arrest her. The leader. More surgical.

LIEUTENANT. Just remember: Fires spread. There are lots of empty chairs, all over this valley, all over this country, ready for kindling. A lot of people are watching.

CAPTAIN. Watching me.

LIEUTENANT. Watching us.

CAPTAIN. Thank you.

Perhaps, at some point in the future, you and I can spend a social evening together. In the city. Find some attractive women. The women around here are remarkably ugly.

LIEUTENANT. And remarkably stubborn. (*They laugh.*)

LIEUTENANT. Finally, there's no reasoning with them. That crazy old woman.

CAPTAIN. Oh, I'll reason with her. I will show her how irresistibly persuasive reason can be. I'll break her fucking back.

LIEUTENANT. I'll go and get her.

CAPTAIN. And pick up her grandson while you're at it.

Little pause.

If you'd rather not do the boy I can send Emmanuel.

LIEUTENANT. That's – considerate of you, Captain.

CAPTAIN. It's nothing.

I had a special mother.

She taught me, as a child, to always be my brother's keeper.

LIEUTENANT. So did mine.

Scene 25

The Fuentes's house. The yard is strewn with the family's belongings. FIDELIA sits in the rubble. ALONSO sits on the steps of the house, holding the baby. YANINA stands looking at the ruination. She goes to ALONSO, *holds his head, pats him tenderly then gently takes the baby from his arms.* ALONSO *begins to cry quietly.* YANINA *walks the baby to the middle of the yard.*

ALEXANDRA *enters, breathing very hard, her hair wild, her clothes torn and her face bloody.*

ALEXANDRA. I'll never see him again.

YANINA. Don't say that.

He's too smart for them, he . . .

Fidelia?

FIDELIA *doesn't move.*

ALEXANDRA. Fidelia, Yani's talking to you.

YANINA. Take your uncle inside, Fidelia. He needs . . . to go inside.

FIDELIA *gets up. She and* ALEXANDRA *look at each other. Then* FIDELIA *takes* ALONSO *by the hand and leads him in.*

YANINA. You're a mess.

ALEXANDRA. Is the baby alright?

YANINA. Smiling.

You'll get him back. We'll co-operate. They'll bring him back, they wouldn't hurt a boy.

ALONSO *comes in.*

ALONSO. Yanina . . . ?

YANINA (*a beat, she goes to him, then says to* ALEXANDRA). All night he thrashes and he cries. His beautiful back is just scars.

Who are the men who did this to you, who do you see in your dreams? When will they pay for your scarring? I want to go into your dreams and drag those men out from the dark into daylight. I feel such . . . Rage. I think it will kill me.

FIDELIA *enters.*

ALEXANDRA. When they took Emiliano away I thought if
I keep quiet and still they won't hurt him and he'll come
back, someday, safe. They made me dance their steps every
day ever since. Quiet and still, we all thought that, but
there's always someone else they can take. I want my boy
safe, but . . . We have to say an end to this. Finally, finally
an end. They have to give us what's ours, living, dead, give
us the men back, and if the men are murdered then give us
their murderers. It's justice.

YANINA. Alonso. I'm going down to be with the women at
the river.

ALONSO. Yani . . .

YANINA. If there was time, I could heal this. But there's no
time now.

(*To* FIDELIA.) Take the baby.

YANINA *goes to* FIDELIA, *who backs away a step.*
YANINA *hands her the baby, and then picks up a chair
lying in the yard and begins to exit.*

FIDELIA. Mama . . . ?

ALEXANDRA. I'm going too.

FIDELIA. I want to go with you.

ALEXANDRA. Someone has to watch the baby.

FIDELIA. Alonso can do that.

ALEXANDRA. No. I don't think Alonso can.

FIDELIA. It's not my baby. I don't know what to do with him.
If he gets upset . . .

ALEXANDRA. Feed him.

FIDELIA. If there's no food?

ALEXANDRA. Talk to him. Tell him stories.

FIDELIA. Mama, please don't go.

ALEXANDRA. Carry me with you, be a home for me.

She picks up the remaining chair.

I am your mother.

ALEXANDRA *and* YANINA *put their arms around each other and go out of the yard to the river.* FIDELIA *watches them leave.*

Scene 26

In a cell. The CAPTAIN, EMMANUEL *and* SOFIA. *It's almost completely dark. There is a sound of water, dripping.*

CAPTAIN. Talk. Talk, you old savage. You think this is heroic? You think anyone even knows this is. happening? I will load your body and their bodies onto the back of a wagon and dump you in a deep pit somewhere and after the quicklime and the dirt that's all, that's it, that's all that it will be. Just nothing. End it. You can. End it or I'll end it.

(*To* EMMANUEL.) Lights, goddamit, do you think I'm a fucking bat?

EMMANUEL *turns on the lights. Everyone blinks.*

Bring in the boy.

SOFIA *reacts.*

Aha. She moves.

EMMANUEL *brings in* ALEXIS. *His hands are tied behind him, he has a stained canvas hood over his head, his shirt is ripped and one shoulder is bloody and obviously dislocated.*

SOFIA. He's a boy.

CAPTAIN. He's a man. This is as big as he gets.

The CAPTAIN *clamps his hand on* ALEXIS' *torn shoulder.* ALEXIS *almost screams.*

SOFIA. He can't help you.

CAPTAIN. But he's already got you talking. He's almost a miracle, this boy.

Pause.

Send the women to their homes. Co-operate or he'll go off
into the darkest corner of the most godforsaken hell-hole
prison, sure as there's a God in heaven he will, and then. . . .

You hear me? You will never see this – boy again. You hear
me? We will hurt him.

ALEXIS. Grandma . . . ?

SOFIA. Captain, do you have children, Captain?

A favour, in the name of your children.

I need a few minutes with him alone.

To say good-bye.

Pause.

CAPTAIN. Mother of God . . .

You're insane, this boy's alive and you can keep him alive,
feel, feel . . .

He grabs her hand, forces it to ALEXIS' *chest, over his
heart.*

He's alive. Feel his heart?

She keeps her hand on his heart. Pause. The CAPTAIN
slaps her hand away.

What do I have to do to get you to go to the river?

SOFIA. We want the men to come home. All of them. You
took them living we want them back living. If they're dead,
we want to bury them.

CAPTAIN. But I offered you that, I . . .

SOFIA. And after that we want the killers punished. This is
what we all want. All of us. By the river.

Little pause.

CAPTAIN. The tragedy of this country is . . . that it doesn't
have to be dry and barren, it's waiting to blossom, it wants
to be green but . . . no one understands that you move
forward in steps, not all at once, and if you ask too much
you wind up with nothing but dust. This boy . . . could learn
to read. He could vote, he could become . . . something

good for his country, he could do that, a citizen. His pain, his ugly death . . . is your dream for him, not mine.

The CAPTAIN *unholsters his gun, holds it near* ALEXIS' *head.*

CAPTAIN. Ask her to save your life. Ask her. ASK HER!

He rips off the hood. ALEXIS *closes his eyes, stands swaying.*

ALEXIS. Grandma.

Silence.

SOFIA. A few minutes. (*Pause.*)

CAPTAIN. What do I get if I give you that?

SOFIA. Maybe some peace. You'll need it. Later. Peace.

CAPTAIN. I'm not granting any more requests. You have nothing to say to him anyway.

He cocks the trigger.

SOFIA. Could I touch him?

CAPTAIN. What for?

SOFIA. Please.

Little pause.

CAPTAIN. You tire me, woman.

Indicates with his head that she can touch ALEXIS. SOFIA *approaches her grandson, touches his heart again. There is a moment where nothing happens, and then the lights change suddenly.* SOFIA *and* ALEXIS *are alone.*

SOFIA. Can you hear me?

ALEXIS. Yes.

SOFIA. They can't hear us, my little man.

I can't protect you, my baby. Do you understand why?

ALEXIS. No.

SOFIA. Do you forgive me?

Little pause.

ALEXIS. Yes.

SOFIA. I have something to tell you.

There are villages of the living and villages of the dead, surrounding us always. Press up against the wall. Behind you. There's a hand in the stone. Reach for it, hold it.

ALEXIS. I'm scared, I . . .

SOFIA. Yes yes, the hand is there. Do you feel it?

ALEXIS. I don't feel anything.

SOFIA. It's your father. You know his hand.

ALEXIS. Yes.

SOFIA. It's a strong hand. It's so gentle for you. So you can be brave. For the one who comes after you, for the ones who come after. People like us don't die. We will be there in the stones of the wall, you and I and the many others, we will be there together, my little man, my baby, till the walls come down.

The lights return, the CAPTAIN *takes her hand from the boy's chest. He looks at* SOFIA.

CAPTAIN. God forgive you. God forgive us all.

A blackout. First one gunshot, then another. Lights up immediately. FIDELIA *and the baby. Below them, at the river, the* WOMEN *and the soldiers gather.*

Scene 27

FIDELIA (*to the baby*). You must learn how to talk. You'll need to talk. There are things you'll have to tell.

But if you decide never to speak, your stories will get told anyway. There are stories that cry out to be told and if the words aren't there they will seep through the skin.

The wind carries them, the smoke does, the river does, the words of the story will find their way, from the farthest, loneliest places, to places where there are people willing to hear . . .

I can wait. I can wait for you to speak. I'm patient. I can wait a long time.

She exits.

Brilliant sunlight by the river. The WOMEN; *opposite them, many soldiers, heavily armed. The* CAPTAIN *and* EMMANUEL, *waiting. The* LIEUTENANT *arrives.*

CAPTAIN. This country's hopeless. They'll have to depopulate it, the whole country and bring in other people, people from outside, people with some other kind of mind.

Pause. The CAPTAIN *looks at the* WOMEN.

LIEUTENANT. Perhaps you'd rather I gave the order, sir?

CAPTAIN. I can do that.

The soldiers draw their rifle bolts, assume positions.

Women: This is your last chance. Go to your homes. Obey, or I will signal my men to move you. They will use as much force as is necessary.

Little pause.

Men: I want the riverbank cleared.

The CAPTAIN *looks again at the* WOMEN; *they look at him. There is suddenly the loud cry of an animal, a blackbird or . . . Everyone, the* WOMEN, *the soldiers, looks up. Then back down, because the river is beginning to sound again. The* WOMEN *move to the river, silently, then go into the water and carry a body out onto the riverbank. They advance towards the soldiers, then stop. They look at each other. Then they advance again – perhaps dancing, perhaps singing, perhaps only moving forward, as they rock the body like a newborn child.*

Blackout.

End of play.

Acknowledgments in the Guise of an Afterword

The origins of this play go back twenty years.

I had been forced to leave Chile in 1973 after General Augusto
Pinochet had seized power and had, since then, wandered
through several countries until finally settling down in 1976
in Holland. It was there, in Amsterdam, that the story which
remains at the core of *Widows* first came to me.

I was working on a painful series of poems about the missing,
men and women who, snatched from their homes by the secret
police in the silence of the night, are never heard of again, their
bodies denied to their relatives as if they had never existed.
As I wrote, I could feel myself being turned into a bridge
through which the living and the dead were trying to
communicate, a burial mound where they could meet and
mourn and touch. By allowing the voices of the disappeared
and the families waiting for their return to speak to each other
using my faraway words I was also finding a way of going
back myself to the faraway country where my own body and,
of course, these very words I was writing, were forbidden,
placing myself imaginatively in that place I had escaped, that
story I could not share except as a witness, except as a channel
for those voices which seemed to be taking possession of my
throat.

One night – it was early, just after dinner – I was visited by
an image, almost a hallucination: an old woman by a river,
holding the hand of a body that had just washed up on its
shores. And the certainty that this scene had happened before,
that this was not the first time that river had yielded a dead
man to the arms of that old and twisted woman.

I wrote all night, the same poem over and over again, trying to
hear that woman I had invented and who nevertheless seemed
to have a life of her own, I spent those long dark European

hours trying to drag that woman out of the darkness inside me, the darkness on the other side of the world where she lay trapped in oblivion and indifference, I sat there and tried to understand word for word what she was saying and that so few in the alien world I unwillingly lived in seemed to care about. And by dawn, a new poem, almost like a new born child, was there on the table where we ate our meals and where I also wrote my work back then in exile, that poem which gave origin to *Widows* was waiting for my wife Angélica, always my first reader, to give her opinion.

This was the poem:

What did you say – they found another one?
– I can't hear you – this morning
another one floating
in the river?
talk louder – so you didn't even dare
no one can identify him?
the police said not even his mother
                not even the mother who bore him
                not even she could
they said that?
the other women already tried – I can't understand
                                what you're saying,
they turned him over and looked at his face, his hands
                                they looked at,

                right,
they're all waiting together,
silent, in mourning,
on the riverbank,
they took him out of the water
he's naked
                as the day he was born,
there's a police captain
and they won't leave until I get there?
He doesn't belong to anybody,
you say he doesn't belong to anybody?

                tell them I'm getting dressed,
                I'm leaving now

> *if the captain's the same one as*
>   *last time*
> *he knows*
>   *what will happen.*
>   *that body will have my name*
>   *my son's my husband's*
>   *my father's*
>
>   *name*
> *I'll sign the papers tell them*
>   *tell them I'm on my way,*
>   *wait for me*
> *and don't let that captain touch him*
> *don't let that captain take one step closer*
>   *to him.*

Tell them not to worry:
I can bury my own dead.

So. It was done. The old woman had a presence, she had been given a voice, she was free to roam the earth in that poem and speak her lines. I had done my job. Now it was up to her to do hers.

Except that the old woman was not content with this. In the fictitious universe of poetry she had defied that captain and now she would not leave me alone in my own unfortunately quite existent historical universe of exile.

As the years went by, I could not rid myself of the certainty that there was more, much more, to her story than what I had written, that in the poem I had merely grazed the outer skin of that pain, that fierce determination of hers not to let the captain bury her dead, and that she wanted me to go deeper, she wanted the world to know what happened before, what happened afterwards, she wanted – in brief – to be narrated, told in time, filled with a world and filling it. That old woman wanted a destiny and she would not rest until I had given it to her.

Perhaps she would never have been successful – after all, I cannot dispense that sort of service to every one of the crazed literary creatures who mill around inside me and clamour for the light of day and paper – if she had not formed an alliance with another obsession of mine that was just as difficult to get rid of: the need to be published in my country, to reach the audience that the dictatorship was denying me. I was particularly worried about the young people back in Chile – and in other countries of Latin America, Argentina, Uruguay, Brazil, so many of them suffering the same tyranny, the same armies imposing death and defeat. And I began to wonder oh so slowly if I could not write a novel dealing with the disappeared, telling the story of that old woman and that river and those bodies and that captain, but using a pseudonym, disguising my name and perhaps even, yes, disguising the country where this was happening. A great deal of the horror of Chile was, after all, enhanced by the fact that this sort of tragedy and this sort of resistance had occurred before in history, that we seemed to be repeating, forty years after the Nazi experiments, some of the same endless sorrows and iniquities. What if I were to make up a Danish author who, living under the German occupation of his country, had written this story, a fictitious author who would himself be, I decided, a missing person? What if that story about an old woman by a river in a place like, say, Greece, had been lost all these years and only recently located and now was being published for the first time? What if that novel, supposedly written by that Danish author, happened to be translated into Spanish and sold in Chile? Could the authorities of my country object? How would they know that I was the real author?

Sometime in the summer of 1978, I began to write that novel which I called, from the very beginning, *Widows*. I could not have written of such loss if I had not, at that time, been accompanied by my wife who was pregnant with the boy who was to be our son Joaquín, if I had not lifted my eyes from the page that was taking me into the hell of those women on a riverbank and been unable to see our eldest son Rodrigo playing cheerfully nearby. The joy that I was experiencing was precisely what was being stolen from my protagonists.

And as, in the months that followed, I answered the call of that old woman and gave her a world in which to live, I embarked as well on a different sort of operation, of a less literary kind:

I appealed to those who, in the real world of real frontiers and real censors, could help me fool the dictatorship in Chile. My primary partners in this wild scam turned out to be two fellow writers both of whom are no longer living – and whose affection and loyalty I can now acknowledge. My friend Heinrich Böll, the German Nobel Prize winner, who had already helped Solzhenitzin smuggle his manuscripts out of the repressive Soviet Union, was delighted with the opportunity of assisting a Chilean writer do the reverse and smuggle his manuscript into a country where he could not be published. He would preface the book, Böll said with a twinkle, as we sat drinking tea in his house near Cologne: he would explain to the readers that the son of an unknown Danish author had come to him with his father's long lost novel that the world should now read forty years after its creator's death at the hands of the Nazi secret police. And a month later in Paris the Argentine writer Julio Cortázar who had been like a brother to me in those years of exile, told me that he would gladly and mischievously appear as the 'translator' of the book into Spanish from the French – though of course the text that would be seeing the light of day would be my own original Spanish language version.

All I needed now was for a publisher who brought out books in Chile, Argentina and Spain and had originally shown some enthusiasm for the project when I had mentioned it to him, to give me the green light. But when the man read the manuscript, he demurred. He wasn't ready, he told me, to risk his whole enterprise on this sort of adventure: the military would quickly see through the ruse and then I would be safely out of harm's way, still banished, but he and his employees and his investors would have to suffer Pinochet's displeasure. There is nothing an Army hates more than being made fun of.

So I was left stranded with my old woman on this side of the barrier of fear that still surrounded Chile. She had not managed to surreptitiously infiltrate me back into my country. But, she suggested, the world was still there, as much in need of this story as my country. We should circulate it abroad, wherever we could until that remote day when Chile would be free to receive my words and hers.

I proceeded to publish the novel under my own name. It was no longer necessary to bother Böll and Cortázar. Several foreign editors suggested that I should now make the story more overtly Latin American and militant and denunciatory. Instead, I decided to preserve the framing device of the Danish author and to keep the Greek setting for the story. I did not want readers to feel that this was merely some exotic abuse in lands that they had barely heard of. I wanted them to ask themselves about the connections between my country and theirs, my present and their past, our present and their future. And besides, I had discovered that the distancing of my urgent reality back home, my ability to pretend someone else had written that narrative, had had a liberating effect on it. This allegorical approach helped to solve an artistic dilemma that besieges many authors who deal with contemporary political issues: how to write about matters that have extraordinary documentary weight without being subjected to the grinding jaws of a 'realism' that is often unwilling to depict the complexity of what is truly happening? To give just one example: when I wrote that novel, no bodies of the missing had yet been unearthed, neither in Chile nor elsewhere. If I had written only about what was effectively transpiring in my land, I would have been limited to tracing and copying what history had already materialised. Instead, I imagined a different scenario, one that history was hiding at the moment but which would, in the years to come, reveal itself: I prophesied that the bodies would begin to appear, that nobody could stop the dead from coming home, that the women were bringing them back against silence and oppression and, in effect, as time went by, they began to emerge from the rivers and the mine shafts and the fields and the sands of Chile and Latin America, they came as if from the depths of the imagination of the world. I didn't want to be trapped into reproducing what existed out there. I wanted my literature to explore an alternative future that my imagination could see and that perhaps could someday emerge from reality itself. I also saw my story going beyond mere denunciations of the terrors of a dictatorship, asking questions about memory and gender and betrayal and community and writing itself which should not be subsumed in what seemed to be the political questions the text posed.

This dilemma of how to tell a story that was historical inasmuch as it derived from the suffering of real human beings but that simultaneously had to obey aesthetic and literary laws of representation that demanded freedom from that immediate history, would come back to haunt me in the story's next embodiment, when many years later, one day in 1985, I got a call from Judy James, then with the Mark Taper Forum in Los Angeles, who had been given the novel by my friend Deena Metzger and who thought it cried out to be a play and, eventually she thought, a film.

The old woman inside me agreed. She wanted more people to see her life, to witness how she had not allowed death to dictate that life. She wanted to live again, this time on stage.

Thus began one of the longest and most arduous creative odysseys of my existence. The poem had taken a night to compose and the novel, a year. The play was to bedevil me for almost a decade.

Widows the play had many incarnations. Under the diligent guiding light of my director at the Taper, Bob Egan, and supported with verve by Gordon Davidson, the artistic director of the company, my play went through many rewrites and two major workshops where the actors gave everything of themselves and, in return, showed me no mercy with their questions. I felt that I knew the women of this play, knew who they were, from what despair and loss and ambiguity they acted: it was the men, the military, who ended up being a real enigma, and in those workshops Richard Jordan and René Auberjenois who incarnated the Captain, and Tony Plana, who played the Lieutenant, were particularly helpful. But advice was not enough: I needed to see it fully staged to try and figure out what was wrong. In 1988, Diane and Johnny Simons of the Hip Pocket Theatre in Forth Worth, Texas, premiered a version that had just won a New American Plays Award at the Kennedy Center; and that same summer I went on to get another production starring Tony Musante and directed by Kay Matschullat at the Williamstown Theatre Festival. Reviews and audiences were enthusiastic, but I knew, as I watched the staging, that the play had not yet freed itself from the magic of the novel.

After yet another rewrite and another disappointing reading at the always faithful Taper, Bob Egan and Gordon Davidson proposed in 1989 a different solution: perhaps I needed someone else to come in and collaborate with me. I was sceptical, but the old woman inside me kept nagging, the dead and the missing inside us would not leave either of us alone. So I reluctantly agreed to read some of the plays of the man my friends at the Taper thought could help me bring my vision to fruition. He was a relatively unknown playwright but was bound, they were sure, for great things.

His name was Tony Kushner.

When I read his plays, *A Bright Room Called Day*, and the first draft of an absolutely compelling drama entitled *Angels in America*, I agreed that he was indeed the right person to work with me. Tony's vision might be different from mine, but he was struggling with my same demons of expression, confronting ways in which politics and imagination intersect, how to depict suffering and repression without sinking into hopelessness, how to be colloquial and simultaneously mythical, how to show human resistance and resilience without being propagandistic or doctrinaire, how to recognise that we have the enemy inside and the best people are capable of the most terrible things.

If I deluded myself into believing that I was the bridge the missing had been looking for to enter the world and speak to it, Tony became in effect the bridge I had been looking for to enter the world of theatre and reach the U.S. audience which I had found trouble in connecting to this particular story so removed politically and aesthetically from the typical American tradition. For the next two years, interrupted by several trips of my own back to Chile where I could now go and where we were in the process of ousting Pinochet from power, Tony patiently helped me craft *Widows* into the play it had always promised to be, provided dialogue and characters and rhythm, day after day after day. He is the co-author of this text, its midwife, the hands that helped the play, like a child, to grow. I cannot thank him enough for what he taught me, for his loyalty to the old woman and her family, for his friendship to me and my own family.

And yet, the play which finally opened on the mainstage of the
Mark Taper Forum directed by Bob Egan in 1991 – ten days
after another play of mine, *Death and the Maiden* had its
premiere at the Royal Court in London – was still not exactly
what I wanted. As I watched the performance in Los Angeles,
there was something still missing, something the novel had
possessed and that this play, for all its power, had not yet
managed to achieve. I had no idea what that missing something
could possibly be – only that I might now have strayed too far
from the original vision and that I had to find a way to get
back to it. The text still beckoned me to journey with it for one
last time.

My next few years were filled with *Death and the Maiden* –
and Tony's own stunning success with *Angels in America*; so
neither he nor I found the time or the tranquillity to return to
Widows again. And yet, for me, in the back of my mind, it was
always there, demanding to find its voice and be complete.
This secret dialogue with myself might well have gone on
forever if the Andrew Wylie Agency had not one day received
a call from Ian Brown at the Traverse Theatre: he wanted to
do our play up in Edinburgh. My answer to him – as it had
been to others who had recently inquired about possible new
productions – was that the play needed one more rewrite
before it would be ready. But my agent, Deborah Karl, would
not let me off the hook that easily. She insisted that I should
say yes to the Traverse's offer and force myself once and for
all to finish the play. And she was right: when I concentrated
on the characters and structure again, I discovered the changes
I thought the play required. However, when I met my co-author
for lunch in New York and told him my plans, Tony stated,
with his usual generosity, that I should go ahead without him,
that I had to run this last lap on my own.

And that was how I found myself again writing alone,
wrestling with my solitude and that old woman's affliction,
offering *Widows* one last ritual elaboration, one more labour of
love. Besides a couple of minor alterations, shifts in emphasis,
a heightening of the lyrical and mythical qualities of the
drama, the major modification – one which, in fact, I only
could have accomplished by myself, by going into my own

pain one last time – framed the play with a narrator who is himself, as I had been, an exile who watches, witnesses, suffers the action from afar.

Once the new version of the play toured England in 1996, I discovered, however, that my decision to introduce this enigmatic male figure into the action as an intermediary between the real audience and the mythical characters, turned out to be completely misunderstood and, in fact, counter-productive. Exile might have been at the origin of my relationship with that old woman and her missing loved ones, but spectators almost unanimously felt that such an infiltration distanced them from that tragedy without bringing them any closer to our impure contemporary world.

And so, for this definitive, final version of *Widows* the play, I have decided to eliminate that narrator and trust that the story itself will be strong enough to reach the right audience. Perhaps in its next incarnation – in *Widows* the film, which currently shows signs of soon finding its way into a world in dire need of its message – that narrator will be able to make a reappearance, watch the story as I did from another country, maybe the narrator, unlike the man who writes these words, will be swallowed up by what he is watching, maybe he will suffer the same fate as his characters.

It should be clear by now that this play has arrived at its final published version only because it was supported through two decades by countless men and women who believed in it. Some of those names have been alluded to in these pages. Space does not allow so many deserving others to receive my gratitude here, but they do know who they are. Thanks to you, one and all, for having helped to bring to life a play that needed so many actors and that dealt with issues that are so dark and unyielding and apparently remote.

I have left for the end the most important acknowledgment and recognition of all.

I made up that old woman.

I invented her and her family and that river and that captain who does not know how to deal with her.

If she could come from my imagination, however, it was because she had been placed there, sparked into being, inspired into existence by real women who searched for real bodies in a real world more cruel and inhuman than anything I finally described in my fiction.

Democracy has returned now to Chile and to so many other countries where those widows resisted the military and demanded their men back. Democracy has returned, but many of those women are still waiting for the return of their fathers, their husbands, their brothers, their sons, many of them are still waiting for a river or a god to bring those bodies back from the dead. And the bodies are also waiting, somewhere, are still accusing the men who murdered them, are still waiting for justice to be done, are still demanding to be remembered by a society that is all too willing to forget.

It is to those waiting women, the women who are the hidden and silent storytellers of this tale that came to me as if in a dream twenty years ago, it is to them that *Widows* is finally dedicated.

Ariel Dorfman, October 1997

DEATH AND THE MAIDEN

This play is dedicated to
María Elena Duvauchelle
and
Harold Pinter

Characters

PAULINA SALAS, *around forty years old*

GERARDO ESCOBAR, *her husband, a lawyer, around
    forty-five*

ROBERTO MIRANDA, *a doctor, around fifty*

*The time is the present and the place, a country that is
probably Chile but could be any country that has given itself a
democratic government just after a long period of dictatorship.*

ACT ONE

Scene One

*Sounds of the sea. After midnight. The Escobars's beach house.
A terrace and an ample living/dining room where dinner is laid
out on a table with two chairs. On a sideboard is a cassette
recorder and a lamp. Window walls between the terrace and
the front room, with curtains blowing in the wind. A door from
the terrace leading to a bedroom. PAULINA SALAS is seated
in a chair on the terrace, as if she were drinking in the light
of the moon. The sound of a faraway car can be heard.
She hurriedly stands up, goes to the other room, looks out
the window. The car brakes, its motor still running, the lights
blasting her. She goes to the sideboard, takes out a gun, stops
when the motor is turned off and she hears* GERARDO's
voice.

GERARDO (*voice off*). You sure you don't want to come in?
Just one for the road (*Muffled reply.*) . . . Right then, we'll
get together before I leave. I've gotta be back by . . .
Monday. How about Sunday? (*Muffled reply.*) . . . My wife
makes a margarita that will make your hair stand on end . . .
I really want you to know how much I appreciate . . .
(*Muffled reply.*) See you on Sunday then. (*He laughs.*)

*PAULINA hides the gun away. She stands behind the
curtains. The car drives off, the lights sweeping the room
again.* GERARDO *enters.*

GERARDO. Paulie? Paulina?

He sees PAULINA *hidden behind the curtains. He switches
on a light. She slowly comes out from the curtains.*

Is that . . . ? What're you doing there like that? Sorry that
I took this long to . . . I . . .

PAULINA (*trying not to seem agitated*). And who was that?

GERARDO. It's just that I . . .

PAULINA. Who was it?

GERARDO. . . . had an – no, don't worry, it wasn't anything serious. It's just that the car – luckily a man stopped – just a flat tyre. Paulina, I can't see a thing without . . .

He puts on another lamp and sees the table set.

Poor little love. It must've got cold, right, the –

PAULINA (*very calm, till the end of the scene*). We can heat it up. As long as we've got something to celebrate, that is.

Brief pause.

You do have something to celebrate, Gerardo, don't you?

GERARDO. That depends on you.

Pause. He takes an enormous nail out of his jacket pocket.

You know what this is? This is the son of a bitch that gave me a flat. And do you know what any normal man does when he gets a flat? He goes to the trunk and he gets out the spare. If the spare isn't flat too, that is. If his wife happened to remember to fix the spare, right?

PAULINA. His wife. Always got to be the wife who has to fix everything. You were supposed to fix the spare.

GERARDO. I'm really not in the mood for arguing, but we had agreed that . . .

PAULINA. You were supposed to do it. I take care of the house and you take care of –

GERARDO. You don't want help but afterwards you . . .

PAULINA. – the car at least.

GERARDO. . . . afterwards you complain.

PAULINA. I never complain.

GERARDO. This is an absurd discussion. What're we fighting about? I've already forgotten what we . . .

PAULINA. We're not fighting, darling. You accused me of not fixing your spare . . .

GERARDO. *My* spare?

PAULINA. – and I told you quite reasonably that I –

GERARDO. Hold it right there. Let's clear this thing up here and now. That you didn't fix the spare, *our* spare, that's open to discussion, but there is another little matter. The jack.

PAULINA. What jack?

GERARDO. Right. What jack? Where did you put the car jack? You know, to jack the –

PAULINA. You need a jack to hold up the car?

He embraces her.

GERARDO. Now. What the hell did you do with the jack?

PAULINA. I gave it to mother.

GERARDO (*letting go of her*). To your mother? You *gave* it to your mother?

PAULINA. Loaned it. Yes.

GERARDO. And may I ask why?

PAULINA. You may. Because she needed it.

GERARDO. Whereas I, of course, we . . . You just can't – baby, you simply cannot do this sort of thing.

PAULINA. Mom was driving down south and really needed it, while you . . .

GERARDO. While I can go fuck myself.

PAULINA. No.

GERARDO. Yes. I get a telegram and I have to leave for the city immediately to see the president in what is the most important meeting of my whole life and –

PAULINA. And?

GERARDO. . . . and this son of a bitch of a nail is lying in wait for me, fortunately not on my way there that – and there I was, without a spare and without a jack on the goddamn road.

PAULINA. I knew that you'd find someone to help you out.
Was she pretty at least? Sexy?

GERARDO. I already said it was a man.

PAULINA. You said nothing of the kind.

GERARDO. Why do you always have to suppose there's a
woman . . .

PAULINA. Why indeed? I just can't imagine why.

Brief pause.

Nice? The man who . . .?

GERARDO. Great guy. It's lucky for me that he . . .

PAULINA. You see? I don't know how you do it, but you
always manage to fix things up so that everything turns out
right for you . . . While mom, you can be sure that if she
had a hat some weird person was going to stop and – you
know how mom attracts the craziest sort of –

GERARDO. You can't imagine how ecstatic it makes me to
think of your mother exploring the south with my jack, free
of all worries, while I had to stand there for hours –

PAULINA. No exaggerating now. . .

GERARDO. Forty-five minutes. Exactly forty-five. The cars
passed by as if I didn't exist. You know what I began to do?
I began to move my arms around like a windmill to see if
that way – we've forgotten what solidarity is in this country?
Lucky for me, this man – Roberto Miranda – I invited him
over for a –

PAULINA. I heard you.

GERARDO. How's Sunday?

PAULINA. Sunday's fine.

Brief pause.

GERARDO. As we're going back Monday. At least I am. And
I thought you might want to come with me, shorten these
holidays . . .

PAULINA. So the president named you?

Brief pause.

GERARDO. He named me.

PAULINA. The peak of your career.

GERARDO. I wouldn't call it the peak. I am, after all, the youngest of those he named, right?

PAULINA. Right. When you're minister of justice in a few years' time, that'll be the peak, huh?

GERARDO. That certainly doesn't depend on me.

PAULINA. Did you tell him that?

GERARDO. Who?

PAULINA. Your good Samaritan.

GERARDO. You mean Roberto Miranda? I hardly know the man. Besides, I haven't decided yet if I should . . .

PAULINA. You've decided.

GERARDO. I said I'd answer tomorrow, that I felt extremely honoured but that I needed . . .

PAULINA. The president? You said that to the president?

GERARDO. To the president. That I needed time to think it over.

PAULINA. I don't see what you have to think over. You've made your decision, Gerardo, you know you have. It's what you've been working for all these years, why pretend that . . .

GERARDO. Because first – first you have to say yes.

PAULINA. Well then: yes.

GERARDO. That's not the yes I need.

PAULINA. It's the only yes I've got.

GERARDO. I've heard others.

Brief pause.

If I were to accept, I must know I can count on you, that you don't feel. . . if you were to have a relapse, it could leave me . . .

PAULINA. Vulnerable, yes, it could leave you vulnerable. Stripped. You'd have to take care of me all over again.

GERARDO. That's unfair.

Brief pause.

Are you criticising me because I take care of you?

PAULINA. And that's what you told the president, that your wife might have problems with . . .

Pause.

GERARDO. He doesn't know. Nobody knows. Not even your mother knows.

PAULINA. There are people who know.

GERARDO. I'm not talking about those kinds of people. Nobody in the new government knows. I'm talking about the fact that we never made it public, as you never – as we never denounced the things that they – what they . . .

PAULINA. Only if the result was death, huh?

GERARDO. Paulina, I'm sorry, what do you –

PAULINA. This Commission you're named to. Doesn't it only investigate cases that ended in death?

GERARDO. It's appointed to investigate human rights violations that ended in death or the presumption of death, yes.

PAULINA. Only the most serious cases?

GERARDO. The idea is that if we can throw light on the worst crimes, other abuses will also come to light.

PAULINA. Only the most serious?

GERARDO. Let's say the cases that are beyond – let's say, repair.

PAULINA. Beyond repair. Irreparable, huh?

GERARDO. I don't like to talk about this, Paulina.

PAULINA. I don't like to talk about it either.

GERARDO. But we'll have to talk about it, won't we, you and I? If I'm going to spend the next few months listening to the evidence, relatives and eye-witnesses and survivors – and each time I come back home I – and you wouldn't want me to keep all that to myself. And what if you . . . if you . . .

He takes her in his arms.

If you knew how much I love you. If you knew how it still hurts me.

Brief pause.

PAULINA (*fiercely holding on to him*). Yes. Yes. Yes. Is that the yes that you wanted?

GERARDO. That's the yes that I wanted.

PAULINA. Find out what happened. Find out everything. Promise me that you'll find everything that . . .

GERARDO. Everything. Everything we can. We'll go as far as we . . . (*Pause.*) As we're . . .

PAULINA. Allowed.

GERARDO. Limited, let's say we're limited. But there is so much we can do . . . We'll publish our conclusions. There will be an official report. What happened will be established objectively, so no one will ever be able to deny it, so that our country will never again live through the excesses that . . .

PAULINA. And then?

GERARDO *is silent.*

You hear the relatives of the victims, you denounce the crimes, what happens to the criminals?

GERARDO. That depends on the judges. The courts receive a copy of the evidence and the judges proceed from there to –

PAULINA. The judges? The same judges who never intervened to save one life in seventeen years of dictatorship? Who never accepted a single habeas corpus ever? Judge Peralta who told that poor woman who had come to ask for her missing husband that the man had probably grown tired of her and run off with some other woman? That judge? What did you call him? A judge? A judge?

As she speaks, PAULINA *begins to laugh softly but with increasing hysteria.*

GERARDO. Paulina, Paulina. That's enough. Paulina.

He takes her in his arms. She slowly calms down.

Silly. Silly girl, my baby.

Brief pause.

And what would have happened if you'd had the flat? You there on that road with the cars passing, the lights passing like a train, screaming by, and nobody stopping, did you think of what could have happened to you if you found yourself alone there on the road all of a –

PAULINA. Someone would have stopped. Probably that same – Miranda?

GERARDO. Probably. Not everybody's a son of a bitch.

PAULINA. No . . . Not everybody.

GERARDO. I invited him for a drink on Sunday. What do you think?

PAULINA. Sunday's fine.

Brief pause.

I was frightened. I heard a car. When I looked it wasn't yours.

GERARDO. But there was no danger.

PAULINA. No.

Brief pause.

Gerardo.

You already said yes to the president, didn't you? The truth, Gerardo. Or are you going to start your work on the Commission with a lie?

GERARDO. I didn't want to hurt you.

PAULINA. You told the president you accepted, didn't you? Before you asked me? Didn't you? I need the truth, Gerardo.

GERARDO. Yes. I told him I'd do it. Yes. Before asking you.

Lights go down.

Scene Two

One hour later. Nobody on stage. Only the moonlight, weaker than before, coming in through the windows. Dinner has been cleared away. Sound of the sea beyond. The sound of a car approaching. Then the headlights light up the living room, are switched off, a car door is opened and closed. Someone knocks on the door, first timidly, then more strongly. A lamp is switched on from offstage and is immediately switched off. The knocking on the door gets more insistent. GERARDO *comes into the living room in his pyjamas from the bedroom.*

GERARDO (*to* PAULINA, *who is offstage*). I'm telling you – nothing is going to – all right, all right, love, I'll be careful.

GERARDO *switches on the lamp.*

I'm coming, I'm coming.

He goes to the door and opens it. ROBERTO MIRANDA *is outside.*

Oh, it's you. God, you scared the shit out of me.

ROBERTO. I'm really so sorry for this – intrusion. I thought you'd still be up celebrating.

GERARDO. You must excuse my . . . – do come in.

ROBERTO *enters the house.*

It's just that we still haven't got used to it.

ROBERTO. Used to it?

GERARDO. To democracy. That someone knocks on your door at midnight and it's a friend and not . . .

PAULINA *edges out onto the terrace from where she will be able to hear the men but not see or be seen by them.*

ROBERTO. And not one of these bastards?

GERARDO. And my wife has . . . She's been a bit nervous and . . . So you'll understand that – you'll have to forgive her if she doesn't . . . And if we lower our voices a little . . .

ROBERTO. Of course, of course, it's my fault, I just thought .

GERARDO. Please sit down, please do . . .

ROBERTO. . . . that I'd stop by for a short visit to . . . Okay, but just a minute, no more than – but you must be asking yourself why this sudden visit . . . Well, I was driving back to my beach house.

GERARDO. Excuse me, would you like a drink? Sunday you can have one of my wife's famous margaritas, but I do possess a cognac from the duty free that I –

PAULINA *edges nearer and listens.*

ROBERTO. No, thanks, I . . . Well, a teensy-weensy bit. So I'm listening to the radio in my car and . . . all of a sudden, it hit me. I heard your name on the news, the list of names the president's chosen for his Investigating Commission, and they say Gerardo Escobar, and I said to myself that sounds familiar, but where, who, and it kept going round in my head, and when I reached our house I realised who it was. And I also remembered we'd put your spare tyre in the trunk of my car and that tomorrow you'd need it patched up and also . . . the real real truth is, you want to know the truth?

GERARDO. I can't wait.

ROBERTO. I thought to myself – this man is doing something really essential for the honour of the nation – so the country can shut the door on the divisions and hatreds of the past and I thought here's the last weekend that he's going to be free of worries for – for who knows how many months, right, because you're going to have to go up and down this country of ours listening to thousands of people . . . Don't tell me that –

GERARDO. That's certainly true, but I wouldn't go so far
as to –

ROBERTO. So I thought the least I can do is drive over and
leave him his spare so he won't have to go out to phone for
a taxi or a tow truck – I mean, who has a phone out here.

GERARDO. You're making me feel as if I were –

ROBERTO. No, I am telling you, and this is said straight from
the heart, this Commission is going to help us close an
exceptionally painful chapter in our history, and here I am,
alone this weekend, we've all got to help out – it may be a
teensy-weensy gesture but –

GERARDO. Tomorrow would have been fine.

ROBERTO. Tomorrow? You manage to get to your car –
no spare. Then you have to set out and find me. No, my
friend, – and then I thought I might as well offer to go fix
it with you tomorrow with my jack – which reminds me –
what happened to your jack, did you find out what –

GERARDO. My wife loaned it to her mother.

ROBERTO. To her mother?

GERARDO. You know women. . .

ROBERTO (*laughing*). All too well. The last mystery. We are
going to explore all the frontiers, my friend, and we will
still have that unpredictable female soul. You know what
Nietzsche once wrote – at least I think it was Nietzsche?
That we can never entirely possess that female soul. Or
maybe it wasn't him. Though you can be sure that old
Nietzsche would have if he'd found himself on a weekend
road without a jack.

GERARDO. And without a spare.

ROBERTO. And without a spare. Which clinches it – I really
must go with you and we'll clean up the whole operation in
one morning . . .

GERARDO. I feel that I am imposing.

ROBERTO. I won't hear another word. I happen to like to help people, – I'm a doctor, I told you, didn't I? But don't get it in your head that I only help important people.

GERARDO. If you had known what you were getting into you'd have stomped the accelerator to the floor, huh?

ROBERTO (*laughing*). Through the floor. No, seriously, it's no trouble at all. In fact, it's an honour. In fact, if you want to know the real real truth, look, that's why I came here tonight, to congratulate you, to tell you that . . . You are exactly what this country needs, to be able to find out the truth once and for all . . .

GERARDO. What the country needs is justice, but if we can determine at least part of the truth . . .

ROBERTO. Just what I was about to say. Even if we can't put these people on trial, even if they're covered by this amnesty they gave themselves – at least their names can be published.

GERARDO. Those names are to be kept secret. The Commission is not supposed to identify the authors of crimes or –

ROBERTO. In this country everything finally comes out into the open. Their children, their grandchildren, is it true that you did this, you did what they're accusing you of, and they'll have to lie. They'll say it's slander, it's a communist conspiracy, some such nonsense, but the truth will be written all over them, and their children, their very own children, will feel sorrow for them, disgust and sorrow. It's not like putting them in jail, but . . .

GERARDO. Maybe some day . . .

ROBERTO. Maybe if the citizens of this country get angry enough we may even be able to revoke the amnesty.

GERARDO. You know that's not possible.

ROBERTO. I'm for killing the whole bunch of them, but I can see that . . .

GERARDO. I hate to disagree, Roberto, but in my opinion the
death penalty has never solved any of the –

ROBERTO. Then we're going to have to disagree, Gerardo.
There are people who simply don't deserve to be alive, but
what I was really getting at was that you're going to have
quite a problem . .

GERARDO. More than one. For starters, the Army is going to
fight the Commission all the way. They've told the president
this investigation was an insult, and dangerous, yes,
dangerous, for the new government to be opening old
wounds. But the president went ahead anyway, thank God,
for a moment I thought he'd get cold feet, but we all know
these people are ready to jump on us at the slightest mistake
we make . . .

ROBERTO. Well, that was exactly my point, when you said
that the names wouldn't be known, published, when you –
maybe you're right, maybe we'll finally never know who
these people really were, they form a sort of . . .

GERARDO. Mafia.

ROBERTO. Mafia, yes, a secret brotherhood, nobody gives out
names and they cover each others' backs. The Armed Forces
aren't going to allow their men to give testimony to your
Commission and if you people call them in they'll just
ignore your summons, just say fuck you. Maybe you're
right and this thing about the children and the grandchildren
is nothing but a fantasy. It may not be as easy as I thought,
that's what I was really getting at.

GERARDO. Not that difficult either. The president told me –
and this stays between us, of course –

ROBERTO. Of course.

GERARDO. The President told me that there are people who
are ready to make statements, just so long as their
confidentiality is guaranteed. And once people start talking,
once the confessions begin, the names will pour out like
water. Like you said: in this country we end up knowing
everything.

ROBERTO. I wish I could share your optimism. I'm afraid there are things we'll never know.

GERARDO. We're limited, but not that limited. At the very least we can expect some sort of moral sanction, that's the least . . . As we can't expect justice from the courts . . .

ROBERTO. I hope to God you're right. But it's getting late. Lord, it's two o'clock. Look, I'll be back to pick you up tomorrow, let's say at – how about nine?

GERARDO. Why don't you stay over unless you've got someone waiting for you back at your . . .

ROBERTO. Not a soul.

GERARDO. Well, if you're alone.

ROBERTO. Not alone. My wife and kids have gone off to her mother's of all places and as I hate to fly, and I've got some patients that –

GERARDO. Not at your beach house you don't. So why don't you – ?

ROBERTO. It's very kind of you but I like being by myself, watching the waves, listening to my music. Look, I came to help, not to be a bother. I'll be back tomorrow, say at –

GERARDO. I won't hear of it. You're staying. You're what? You're half an hour away?

ROBERTO. It's around forty minutes by the coast road, but if I –

GERARDO. Not another word. Paulina will be delighted. You'll see the breakfast she'll make for us.

ROBERTO. Now that convinced me. Breakfast! I don't think we even have milk at our beach house. And the real real truth is that I am incredibly tired . . .

PAULINA *quickly returns, through the terrace, to her bedroom.*

GERARDO. I wonder if there's anything else you might . . . ? A toothbrush is really the only thing I think I can't offer you . . .

ROBERTO. Of the two things you never share, my friend, one is your toothbrush.

GERARDO. Right!

ROBERTO. Good night.

Both GERARDO *and* ROBERTO *exit in different directions to their respective bedrooms. A brief pause: silence and moonlight.*

GERARDO (*voice off*). Paulina, love . . . That doctor who helped me out on the road, he's staying the night. Love? He's staying because tomorrow he's going to help me pick up the car. Darling, are you listening?

PAULINA (*off, as if half-asleep*). Yes, my love.

GERARDO (*voice off*). He's a friend. So don't be scared. Tomorrow you can make us a nice breakfast . . .

Only the sound of the sea in the semi-darkness.

Scene Three

A short time later. A cloud passes over the moon. The sound of the sea grows, then recedes. Silence.

PAULINA *comes into the living room.*

By the light of the moon she can be seen going to the drawer and taking out the gun. And some vague articles of clothing which appear to be stockings.

She crosses the living/dining room to the entrance to ROBERTO's *bedroom. She waits for an instant, listening. She goes into the bedroom. A few moments pass. We hear a confusing, muffled sound, followed by a sort of cry. Then silence.*

In the half-light we see her come out of the room. She goes back to her own bedroom door. She opens it, takes a key from the inside of the door, locks it. She returns to the spare bedroom. We see her dragging something in, which resembles a body but we can't be sure. As the scene continues, it can be

*seen that it is a body. She moves a chair and hoists the body
onto it, ties it to the chair. She goes into the spare room,
returns with what seems to be* ROBERTO*'s jacket, takes a
set of car keys from it. She starts to leave the house. Stops.
Turns back to look at the body which is now clearly that of*
ROBERTO. *She takes off her panties, stuffs it into*
ROBERTO*'s mouth.*

PAULINA *leaves the house. We hear the sound of* ROBERTO*'s
car. When the car's headlights are turned on, they sweep the
scene and that stark brutal shot of light clearly reveals*
ROBERTO MIRANDA *tied with ropes to one of the chairs,
totally unconscious, and with his mouth gagged. The car
leaves. Darkness.*

Scene Four

Before dawn. ROBERTO *opens his eyes. He tries to get up and
realises that he is tied. He begins to roll over and desperately
tries to free himself.* PAULINA *is sitting in front of him with
her gun.* ROBERTO *looks at her with a terrorised expression
in his eyes.*

PAULINA (*very calm*). Good morning, Doctor. . . Miranda,
isn't it? Doctor Miranda.

*She shows him the gun and points it playfully in his
direction.*

I had a chum from the university, name of Miranda, Ana
Maria Miranda, you wouldn't be related to the Mirandas of
San Esteban, would you? She had quite a mind. A marvellous
retentive memory, we used to call her our little encyclopedia.
I have no idea what became of her. She probably finished
her medical studies, became a doctor, just like you.

I didn't get my diploma . . . I didn't get too far with my
studies, Doctor Miranda. Let's see if you can guess why
I didn't get my diploma, I'm pretty sure that it won't
take a colossal effort of the imagination on your part to
guess why.

Luckily there was Gerardo. He was – well, I wouldn't
exactly say he was waiting for me – but let's say that he still
loved me, so I never had to go back to the university. Lucky
for me, because I felt a – well, phobia wouldn't be the right
word, a certain apprehension – about medicine. I wasn't so
sure about my chosen profession. But life is never over till
it's over, as they say. That's why I'm wondering whether it
might not be a good idea to sign up again – you know, ask
that I be readmitted. I read the other day, now that the
military aren't in charge anymore, that the university has
begun to allow the students who were kicked out to apply
for readmittance.

But here I am chatting away when I'm supposed to make
breakfast, aren't I, a nice breakfast? Now you like – let's
see, ham sandwiches, wasn't it? Ham sandwiches with
mayonnaise. We haven't got mayonnaise, but we do have
ham. Gerardo also likes ham. I'll get to know your other
tastes. Sorry about the mayonnaise. I hope you don't mind
that this must remain, for the moment, a monologue. You'll
have your say, Doctor, you can be sure of that. I just don't
want to remove this – gag, you call it, don't you? – at least
not till Gerardo wakes up. But I should be getting him up.
Did I tell you I phoned the garage from the pay phone?
They'll be here soon.

She goes to the bedroom door, unlocks it, opens it.

The real real truth is that you look slightly bored.

Takes a cassette out of her pocket.

I took this out of your car – I took the liberty – what if we
listen to some Schubert while I make breakfast, a nice
breakfast, Doctor? *Death and the Maiden*?

*She puts it into the cassette player. We begin to hear
Schubert's quartet* Death and the Maiden.

D'you know how long it's been since I last listened to this
quartet? If it's on the radio, I turn it off, I even try not to
go out much, though Gerardo has all these social events
he's got to attend and if they ever name him minister we're
going to live running around shaking hands and smiling

at perfect strangers, but I always pray they won't put on Schubert. One night we were dining with – they were extremely important people, and our hostess happened to put Schubert on, a piano sonata, and I thought, do I switch it off or do I leave, but my body decided for me, I felt extremely ill right then and there and Gerardo had to take me home, so we left them there listening to Schubert and nobody knew what had made me ill, so I pray they won't play that anywhere I go, any Schubert at all, strange isn't it, when he used to be, and I would say, yes I really would say, he's still my favourite composer, such a sad, noble sense of life. But I always promised myself a time would come to recover him, bring him back from the grave so to speak, and just sitting here listening to him with you I know that I was right, that I'm – so many things that are going to change from now on, right? To think I was on the verge of throwing my whole Schubert collection out, crazy!

(*Raising her voice, to* GERARDO.) Isn't this quartet marvellous, my love?

(*To* ROBERTO.) And now I'll be able to listen to my Schubert again, even go to a concert like we used to. Did you know that Schubert was homosexual? But of course you do, you're the one who kept repeating it over and over again while you played *Death and the Maiden*. Is this the very cassette, Doctor, or do you buy a new one every year to keep the sound pure?

GERARDO *enters from the bedroom, still sleepy.*

Good morning, my darling. Sorry breakfast isn't ready yet.

Upon seeing GERARDO, ROBERTO *makes desperate efforts to untie himself.* GERARDO *watches the scene with total astonishment.*

GERARDO. Paulina! What is this? What in the name of . . . Roberto . . . Doctor Miranda.

He moves toward ROBERTO.

PAULINA. Don't touch him.

GERARDO. What?

PAULINA (*threatening him with the gun*). Don't touch him.

GERARDO. What the hell is going on here, what kind of madness is –

PAULINA. It's him.

GERARDO. Put . . . put that gun down.

PAULINA. It's him.

GERARDO. Who?

PAULINA. It's the doctor.

GERARDO. What doctor?

PAULINA. The doctor who played Schubert.

GERARDO. The doctor who played Schubert.

PAULINA. That doctor.

GERARDO. How do you know?

PAULINA. The voice.

GERARDO. But weren't you – you told me – what you told me was all through those weeks . . .

PAULINA. Blindfolded, yes. But I could still hear.

GERARDO. You're sick.

PAULINA. I'm not sick.

GERARDO. You're sick.

PAULINA. All right then, I'm sick. But I can be sick and recognise a voice. Besides, when we lose one of our faculties, the others compensate, they get sharper. Right, Doctor Miranda?

GERARDO. A vague memory of someone's voice is not proof of anything, Paulina, it is not incontrovertible –

PAULINA. It's his voice. I recognised it as soon as he came in here last night. The way he laughs. Certain phrases he uses.

GERARDO. But that's not . . .

PAULINA. It may be a teensy-weensy thing, but it's enough for me. During all these years not an hour has passed that

I haven't heard it, that same voice, next to me, next to my ear, that voice mixed with saliva, you think I'd forget a voice like his?

Imitating the voice of ROBERTO, *then of a man.*

'Give her a bit more. This bitch can take a bit more. Give it to her.'

'You sure, Doctor? What if the cunt dies on us?'

'She's not even near fainting. Give it to her, up another notch.'

GERARDO. Paulina, I'm asking you to please give me that gun.

PAULINA. No.

GERARDO. While you point it at me, there is no possible dialogue.

PAULINA. On the contrary, as soon as I stop pointing it at you, all dialogue will automatically terminate. If I put it down you'll use your strength to win the argument.

GERARDO. Paulina, I want you to know that what you are doing is going to have serious consequences.

PAULINA. Serious, huh? Irreparable, huh?

GERARDO. Yes, it could be – irreparable. Doctor Miranda, I have to ask your forgiveness for – my wife has been –

PAULINA. Don't you dare ask forgiveness from that piece of shit. Do you see that hand, that hand over there –

GERARDO. Untie him, Paulina.

PAULINA. No.

GERARDO. Then I will.

He moves toward ROBERTO. *Suddenly, a shot from* PAULINA*'s gun rings out. It's clear that she does not know how to fire the weapon, because she is as surprised as both men are, recoiling from the shot.* GERARDO *takes a step backward and* ROBERTO *looks desperate.*

GERARDO. Don't shoot, Paulie. Don't shoot that thing off again. Give me that gun.

Silence.

You can't do this.

PAULINA. When are you going to stop telling me what I can and can't do. 'You can't do this, you can do that, you can't do this.' I did it.

GERARDO. You did this to this man, whose only fault that we know of – the only thing you can accuse him of in front of a judge –

PAULINA *laughs derisively.*

– yes, a judge, yes, however corrupt, venal, cowardly – the only thing you could accuse him of is of stopping on the road to help someone who was in trouble, and bring me home and then offer to –

PAULINA. I almost forgot. The man from the garage will be here any minute.

GERARDO. What?

PAULINA. When I went to hide your good Samaritan's car early this morning, I stopped at a public phone and let them know we need them early. So you better get dressed. They must be about to arrive.

GERARDO. Please, Paulina, could we start being reasonable, start acting as if –

PAULINA. You be reasonable. They never did anything to you.

GERARDO. They did things, of course they did things – but we're not competing for some horror prize here, damn it – let's try and be reasonable. Even if this man was the doctor of those terrible events – he isn't, there's no reason why he should be, but let's say he was – even in that case, what right do you have to bind him like this, baby, look at what you're doing, Paulina, think of the consequences of –

The motor of a truck is heard outside. PAULINA *runs to the door, half opens it and shouts out.*

PAULINA. He's coming, he's coming.

She shuts the door, locks it, closes the curtains and looks at GERARDO.

Get dressed, quick. It's the tow truck. The spare's outside. I also took his jack.

GERARDO. You're stealing his jack?

PAULINA. That way mother can keep ours.

Brief pause.

GERARDO. Have you thought I could go to the police?

PAULINA. I doubt you'd do that. You believe too much in your own powers of persuasion. Besides you know that if the police do show their noses here I'll put a bullet straight through this man's head. You do know that, don't you? And then I'll put the gun in my mouth and pull the trigger.

GERARDO. Oh my baby, my baby. You're – unrecognisable. How can you possibly be this way, talk this way?

PAULINA. Explain to my husband, Doctor Miranda, what you did to me so I would be this – crazy.

GERARDO. Paulina. I want you to tell me exactly what it is you intend to do?

PAULINA. Not me. You and me. We're going to put him on trial, Gerardo, this doctor. Right here. Today. You and me. Or is your famous Investigating Commission going to do it?

Lights go down.

End of Act One.

ACT TWO

Scene One

Midday. ROBERTO *is still in the same position,* PAULINA *with her back to him, looking outward to the window and the sea, rocking herself gently as she speaks to him.*

PAULINA. And when they let me go – d'you know where I went? I couldn't go home to my parents – they were so pro-military that at that time I had broken off all diplomatic relations with them, I'd see mother only once in a long while . . . Isn't this bizarre, that I should be telling you all this as if you were my confessor, when there are things I've never told Gerardo, or my sister, certainly not my mother. She'd die if she knew what I've really got in my head. Whereas I can tell you exactly what I feel, what I felt when they let me go. That night . . . well, you don't need me to describe what state I was in, you gave me a quite thorough inspection before I was released, didn't you? We're rather cosy here, aren't we, like this? Like two old pensioners sitting on a bench in the sun.

ROBERTO *makes a gesture, as if he wanted to speak or untie himself.*

Hungry? Things aren't that bad. You'll just have to be patient until Gerardo comes.

Imitating a man's voice.

'You hungry? You wanna eat? I'll give you something to eat, sweet cunt, I'll give you something big and filling so you can forget you're hungry.'

Her own voice.

You don't know anything about Gerardo, do you? – I mean you never knew a thing. I never breathed his name. Your – your colleagues, they'd ask me, of course. 'With that twat, little lady, don't tell me you haven't got someone to fuck

you, huh? Come on, just tell us who's been fucking you,
little lady.' But I never gave them Gerardo's name. Strange
how things turn out. If I had mentioned Gerardo, he
wouldn't have been named to any Investigating
Commission, but would have been one of the names that
some other lawyer was investigating. And I would be in
front of that Commission to tell them how I met Gerardo –
in fact I met him just after the military coup, helping people
seek asylum in embassies – saving lives with Gerardo,
smuggling people out of the country so they wouldn't be
killed. I was wild and fearless, willing to do anything,
I can't believe that I didn't have an ounce of fear in my
whole body at that time. But I am really getting off target.
That night they let me go, well, I went to Gerardo's house,
I knocked on the door, over and over, just like you did last
night, and when Gerardo finally answered, he looked
agitated, his hair was dishevelled –

*The sound of a car outside.Then a car door opening and
closing.* PAULINA *goes to the table and takes the gun in
her hand.* GERARDO *enters.*

How did it go? Was the flat easy to fix?

GERARDO. Paulina, you are going to listen to me.

PAULINA. Of course I'm going to listen to you. Haven't I
always listened to you?

GERARDO. I want you to sit down and I want you to really
listen to me.

PAULINA *sits down.*

You know that I have spent a good part of my life defending
the law. If there was one thing that revolted me in the past
regime –

PAULINA. You can call them fascists . . .

GERARDO. Don't interrupt. If something revolted me about
them it was that they accused so many men and women,
that they forged evidence and ignored evidence and did not
give the accused any chance of defending themselves, so

even if this man committed genocide on a daily basis, he
has the right to defend himself.

PAULINA. But I have no intention of denying him that right,
Gerardo. I'll give you all the time you need to speak to your
client, in private. I was just waiting for you to come back,
that's all, so we could begin this in an orderly official
fashion.

She gestures to GERARDO, *who takes the gag off*
ROBERTO. *Then she indicates the cassette recorder.*

You should know, Doctor, that everything you say will be
recorded here.

GERARDO. My God, Paulina, shut up! Let him say what
he . . .

Brief pause. PAULINA *switches on the recorder.*

ROBERTO (*coughs, then in a rough, hoarse voice*). Water.

GERARDO. What?

PAULINA. He wants water, Gerardo.

GERARDO *rushes to fill a glass with water and brings it to*
ROBERTO, *giving it to him to drink.* ROBERTO *drinks it
down noisily.*

PAULINA. Nothing like good fresh water, eh, Doctor? Beats
drinking your own piss.

ROBERTO. Escobar. This is inexcusable. I will never forgive
you as long as I live.

PAULINA. Hold on, hold on. Stop right there, Doctor. Let's
see if this thing is working.

She presses some buttons and then we hear ROBERTO's
voice.

ROBERTO'S VOICE FROM THE CASSETTE. Escobar. This
is inexcusable. I will never forgive you as long as I live.

PAULINA'S VOICE FROM THE CASSETTE. Hold on, hold
on. Stop right there, Doctor. Let's see.

PAULINA *stops the recorder.*

PAULINA. Ready. It's recording everything marvellously. We already have a statement about forgiveness. It is Doctor Miranda's opinion that it is inexcusable – that he could never forgive as long as he lives – tying someone up for a few hours, holding that person without the right to speak for a few hours. Agreed. More?

She presses another button.

ROBERTO. I do not know you, madam. I have never seen you before in my life. But I can tell you this: you are extremely ill, almost prototypically schizoid. But you, Escobar, you, sir, are not ill. You're a lawyer, a defender of human rights, a man who has been persecuted by the former military government, as I was myself, and your case is different, you are responsible for what you do and what you must do is untie me immediately. And I want you to know that every minute that passes makes you more of an accomplice to this abuse and that you will therefore have to pay the consequences of –

PAULINA (*puts the gun to his temple*). Who are you threatening?

ROBERTO. I wasn't –

PAULINA. Threatening, yes you were. Let's get this clear, Doctor. Threat time is over. Out there you bastards may still give the orders, but in here, for now, I'm in command. Now is that clear?

ROBERTO. I've got to go to the bathroom.

PAULINA. Piss or shit?

GERARDO. My God, Paulina! Doctor Miranda, she has never spoken like this in her life.

PAULINA. The Doctor's used to this sort of language . . . Come on, Doctor. Front or rear?

ROBERTO. Standing up.

PAULINA. Untie his legs, Gerardo. I'll take him.

GERARDO. Of course not. I'll take him.

PAULINA. I'll do it. Don't look at me like that. It's not as if
it's the first time he's going to take his – instrument out in
front of me, Gerardo. Come on, Doctor. Stand up. I don't
want you pissing all over my rug.

GERARDO *unties the legs. Slowly, painfully,* ROBERTO
limps towards the bathroom, with PAULINA *sticking the
gun in his back.* GERARDO *turns off the cassette recorder.*
PAULINA *goes out with* ROBERTO. *After a few instants,
we can hear the sounds of urination and then flushing.
Meanwhile,* GERARDO *has been pacing nervously.*
PAULINA *returns with* ROBERTO.

PAULINA. Tie him up again.

GERARDO *begins to tie up* ROBERTO*'s legs.*

Tighter, Gerardo!

GERARDO. Paulina, this is intolerable. I must talk with you.

PAULINA. And who's stopping you?

GERARDO. Alone.

PAULINA. Why? The doctor used to discuss everything in my
presence, they –

GERARDO. Dear, dear Paulie, please, don't be so difficult.
I want to talk to you where we have some privacy.

GERARDO *and* PAULINA *go out onto the terrace. During
their conversation,* ROBERTO *slowly manages to loosen his
leg bonds.*

What are you trying to do? What are you trying to do,
woman, with these insane acts?

PAULINA. I already told you – put him on trial.

GERARDO. Put him on trial, what does that mean, put him on
trial? We can't use their methods. We're different. To seek
vengeance in this fashion is not –

PAULINA. This is not vengeance. I'm giving him all the
guarantees he never gave me. Not one, him and his –
colleagues.

GERARDO. And his – colleagues – are you going to kidnap them and bring them here and tie them up and . . .

PAULINA. I'd have to know their names for that, wouldn't I?

GERARDO. – and then you're going to . . .

PAULINA. Kill them? Kill him? As he didn't kill me, I think it wouldn't be fair to –

GERARDO. It's good to know that, Paulina, because you would have to kill me too, I'm warning you that if you intend to kill him, you're going to have to kill me first.

PAULINA. Would you mind calming down? I haven't the slightest intention of killing him. And certainly not you . . . But as usual, you don't believe me.

GERARDO. But then, what are you going to do to him? With him? You're going to – what? What are you going to – and all this because fifteen years ago someone . . .

PAULINA. Someone what? . . . what did they do to me, Gerardo. Say it.

Brief pause.

You never wanted to say it. Say it now. They . . .

GERARDO. If you didn't say it, how was I going to?

PAULINA. Say it now.

GERARDO. I only know what you told me that first night, when . . .

PAULINA. They . . .

GERARDO. They . . .

PAULINA. Tell me, tell me.

GERARDO. They – tortured you. Now you say it.

PAULINA. They tortured me. And what else? What else did they do to me, Gerardo?

GERARDO *goes to her, takes her in his arms.*

GERARDO (*whispering to her*). They raped you.

PAULINA. How many times?

GERARDO. More than once.

PAULINA. How many times?

GERARDO. You never said. I didn't count, you said.

PAULINA. It's not true.

GERARDO. What's not true?

PAULINA. That I didn't count. I always kept count. I know
how many times.

Brief pause.

And that night, Gerardo, when I came to you, when I told
you, when I started to tell you, what did you swear you'd
do to them when you found them? 'Some day, my love,
we're going to put these bastards on trial. Your eyes will be
able to rove' – I remember the exact phrase, because it
seemed, poetic – 'your eyes will be able to rove over each
one of their faces while they listen to your story. We'll do
it, you'll see that we will.' So now, darling, tell me who do
I go to now?

GERARDO. That was fifteen years ago.

PAULINA. Tell me who's supposed to listen to my accusations
against this doctor, who, Gerardo? Your Commission?

GERARDO. *My* Commission? What Commission? Thanks to
you, we may not even be able to investigate all the other
crimes that – and I'm going to have to resign.

PAULINA. Always so melodramatic. Your brow gets all
furrowed up with wrinkles that make you look ten years
older. And then people will see your photograph in the
newspaper and won't believe that you're the youngest
member of the Commission.

GERARDO. Are you deaf? I just told you I'm going to have
to resign.

PAULINA. I don't see why.

GERARDO. You don't see why, but all the rest of the country
will see why, especially those who don't want any kind of
investigation of the past will see why. A member of the

president's Commission, who should be showing exemplary
signs of moderation and equanimity –

PAULINA. We're going to suffocate from so much equanimity!

GERARDO. – and objectivity, that this very person has
allowed an innocent human being to be bound and tormented
in his house – do you know how the newspapers that served
the dictatorship, do you know how they'll use this episode
to undermine and perhaps even destroy the Commission?

Brief pause.

Do you want these people back in power? You want to scare
them so they come back to make sure we don't harm them?
You want the times back when these people decided our life
and our death? Because if that's what you want, that's what
you're going to get. Free the man, Paulina. Apologise for
the mistake and free him. I've spoken to him, politically he
seems to be a man we can trust or so it –

PAULINA. Oh, my little man, you do fall for every trick in the
book, don't you? Gerardo, you have my promise, as solemn
as it can be, that this private trial will not affect you or the
Commission. Do you really think I'd do anything to trouble
the Commission, stop you from finding out where the
bodies of the missing prisoners are, how people were
executed, where they're buried. But the members of the
Commission only deal with the dead, with those who can't
speak. And I can speak – it's been years since I murmured
even a word, I haven't opened my mouth to even whisper a
breath of what I'm thinking, years living in terror of my
own . . . but I'm not dead, I thought I was but I'm not and
I can speak, damn it – so for God's sake let me have my say
and you go ahead with your Commission and believe me
when I tell you that none of this is going to be made public.

GERARDO. Even in that case – I have to resign no matter
what, and the sooner, the better.

PAULINA. You'd have to resign even if no one knew about
this?

GERARDO. Yes.

PAULINA. Because of your mad wife, who was mad because
she stayed silent and is now mad because she can speak?

GERARDO. Among other reasons, yes, that's so, if the truth
still matters to you.

PAULINA. The real real truth, huh?

Brief pause.

Could you wait just a sec.

She goes into the other room and discovers ROBERTO
*about to free himself. When he sees her, he stops
immediately.* PAULINA *ties him up again, while her voice
assumes male tones.*

'Hey, don't you like our hospitality? Want to leave so soon,
bitch? You're not going to have such a good time outside
as you're having with me, sweetie. Tell me you'll miss me.
At least tell me that.'

PAULINA *begins to slowly pass her hands up and down*
ROBERTO*'s body, almost as if she were caressing it. Then
she goes back to the terrace.*

PAULINA. It's not only the voice I recognise, Gerardo. I also
recognise the skin. And the smell. Gerardo. I recognise his
skin.

Brief pause.

Suppose I was able to prove beyond a shadow of a doubt
that this doctor of yours is guilty? Would you want me to
set him free anyway?

GERARDO. Yes. If he's guilty, more reason to set him free.
Don't look at me like that. Imagine what would happen if
everyone acted like you did. You satisfy your own personal
passion, you punish on your own, while the other people in
this country with scores of other problems who finally have
a chance to solve some of them, those people can just go
screw themselves – the whole return to democracy can go
screw itself –

PAULINA. Nobody's going to get screwed! Nobody's even
going to know!

GERARDO. The only way to be absolutely sure about that is to kill him and in that case you're the one who's going to get screwed and I'm going to get screwed along with you. Let him go, Paulina. For the good of the country, for our own good.

PAULINA. And me? What I need? Look at me, look at me!

GERARDO. Yes, look at you, love. You're still a prisoner, you stayed there behind with them, locked in that basement. For fifteen years you've done nothing with your life. Not a thing. Look at you, just when we've got the chance to start all over again and you begin to open all the wounds . . . Isn't it time we – ?

PAULINA. Forgot? You're asking me to forget.

GERARDO. Free yourself from them, Paulina, that's what I'm asking.

PAULINA. And let him loose so he can come back in a few years' time?

GERARDO. Let him loose, so he won't come back ever again.

PAULINA. And we see him at the Tavelli and we smile at him, he introduces his lovely wife to us and we smile and we all shake hands and we comment on how warm it is this time of the year and – ?

GERARDO. No need to smile at him but basically yes, that is what we have to do. And start to live, yes.

Brief pause.

PAULINA. Look, Gerardo, I suggest we reach a compromise.

GERARDO. I don't know what you're talking about.

PAULINA. Compromise, an agreement, a negotiation. Everything in this country is done by consensus, isn't it. Isn't that what this transition is all about? They let us have democracy, but they keep control of the economy and of the armed forces? The Commission can investigate the crimes but nobody is punished for them? There's freedom to say anything you want as long as you don't say everything you want?

Brief pause.

So you can see that I'm not that irresponsible or emotional
or . . . sick, I propose that we reach an agreement. You want
this man freed without bodily harm and I want – would you
like to know what I want?

GERARDO. I'd love to know what you want.

PAULINA. When I heard his voice last night, the first thought
that rushed through my head, what I've been thinking all
these years, when you would catch me with a look that you
said was – abstract, fleeting, right? – you know what I was
thinking of? Doing to them, systematically, minute by
minute, instrument by instrument, what they did to me.
Specifically to him, to the doctor . . . Because the others
were so vulgar, so . . . but he would play Schubert, he would
talk about science, he even quoted Nietzsche to me once.

GERARDO. Nietzsche.

PAULINA. I was horrified at myself. That I should have so
much hatred inside – but it was the only way to fall asleep
at night, the only way of going out with you to cocktail
parties in spite of the fact that I couldn't help asking myself
if one of the people there wasn't – perhaps not the exact
same man, but one of those people might be . . . and so as
not to go completely off my rocker and be able to deliver
that Tavelli smile you say I'm going to have to continue to
deliver – well, I would imagine pushing their head into a
bucket of their own shit, or electricity, or when we would
be making love and I could feel the possibility of an orgasm
building, the very idea of currents going through my body
would remind me and then – and then I had to fake it, fake
it so you wouldn't know what I was thinking, so you
wouldn't feel that it was your failure – oh Gerardo.

GERARDO. Oh, my love, my love.

PAULINA. So when I heard his voice, I thought the only
thing I want is to have him raped, have someone fuck him,
that's what I thought, that he should know just once what
it is to . . . And as I can't rape – I thought that it was
a sentence that you would have to carry out.

GERARDO. Don't go on, Paulina.

PAULINA. But then I told myself it would be difficult for you to collaborate in that scheme, after all you do need to have a certain degree of enthusiasm to –

GERARDO. Stop, Paulina.

PAULINA. So I asked myself if we couldn't use a broom. Yes, a broom, Gerardo, you know, a broomstick. But I began to realise that wasn't what I really wanted – something that physical. And you know what conclusion I came to, the only thing I really want?

Brief pause.

I want him to confess. I want him to sit in front of that cassette recorder and tell me what he did – not just to me, everything, to everybody – and then have him write it out in his own handwriting and sign it and I would keep a copy forever – with all the information, the names and data, all the details. That's what I want.

GERARDO. He confesses and you let him go.

PAULINA. I let him go.

GERARDO. And you need nothing more from him?

PAULINA. Not a thing.

Brief pause.

With Miranda's confession in my hand you'd be safe, you could still be on the Commission and he wouldn't dare send his thugs to harm us because he'd know that if harm came to me or to you, his confession would be all over the newspapers the next day.

GERARDO. And you expect me to believe you that you're going to let him go after he's confessed? You expect him to believe that you won't blow his head off as soon as he's confessed?

PAULINA. I don't see that either of you have an alternative. Look, Gerardo, you need to make this sort of scum afraid. Tell him I hid the car because I'm getting ready to kill him. That the only way to dissuade me is for him to confess.

Tell him that nobody knows he came last night, that nobody can ever find him. For his sake, I hope you can convince him.

GERARDO. I have to convince him?

PAULINA. I'd say it's a lot more pleasant than having to fuck him.

GERARDO. There's a problem, of course, you may not have thought of, Paulina. What if he has nothing to confess?

PAULINA. Tell him if he doesn't confess, I'll kill him.

GERARDO. But what if he's not guilty?

PAULINA. I'm in no hurry. Tell him I can wait months for him to confess.

GERARDO. Paulina, you're not listening to me. What can he confess if he's innocent?

PAULINA. If he's innocent? Then he's really screwed.

Lights go down.

Scene Two

Lunch. GERARDO *and* ROBERTO *sit at a table.* ROBERTO *still tied, but this time with his hands in front.* GERARDO *has just finished serving plates of soup.* PAULINA *watches from the terrace. She can see but not hear them.* ROBERTO *and* GERARDO *remain for several silent instants looking at the food.*

GERARDO. You're not hungry, Doctor Miranda?

ROBERTO. Roberto. My name is Roberto. Please treat me with the same familiarity that you – please.

GERARDO. I'd rather speak to you as if you were a client, Doctor Miranda. That will help me out. I think you should eat something.

ROBERTO. I'm not hungry.

GERARDO. Let me . . .

He fills a spoon with soup and feeds ROBERTO *as if he were a baby. During the conversation which follows, he is continually feeding* ROBERTO *and feeding himself:*

ROBERTO. She's mad. You'll have to excuse me for saying this, Gerardo, but your wife . . .

GERARDO. Bread?

ROBERTO. No, thanks.

Brief pause.

She should be receiving some sort of psychiatric treatment for –

GERARDO. To put it brutally, you are her therapy, Doctor.

He cleans ROBERTO's *mouth with a napkin.*

ROBERTO. She's going to kill me.

GERARDO. Unless you confess, she'll kill you.

ROBERTO. But what can I confess? What can I confess if I . . . ?

PAULINA. You may be aware, Doctor, that the secret police used some doctors as – consultants in torture sessions . . .

ROBERTO. The medical association gradually learned of these situations, and looked into them wherever possible.

GERARDO. She is convinced that you are that doctor who . . . And unless you have a way of denying it . . .

ROBERTO. How could I deny it? I'd have to change my voice, prove that this is not my voice – if it's only my voice which damns me, there's no other evidence, nothing that –

GERARDO. And your skin. She mentioned your skin.

ROBERTO. My skin?

GERARDO. And your smell.

ROBERTO. Fantasies of a diseased mind. She could have latched onto any man who came through that door . . .

GERARDO. Unfortunately, you came through that door.

ROBERTO. Look, Gerardo, I'm a quiet man. Anyone can see that I'm incapable of violence – violence of any sort sickens me. I come to my beach house, I wander on the beach, I watch the waves, I hunt for pebbles, I listen to my music – . . .

GERARDO. Schubert?

ROBERTO. Schubert, there's no reason to feel ashamed. I also like Vivaldi and Mozart and Telemann. And I had the stupid idea of bringing Schubert to the beach yesterday. But it was much more stupid to stop for you – Gerardo, I'm in this mess only because I felt sorry for some lunatic waving his arms next to his broken-down car – Look, it's up to you to get me out of here.

GERARDO. I know.

ROBERTO. My ankles hurt, my hands, my back. Couldn't you untie me a little, so –

GERARDO. Roberto, I want to be honest with you. There is only one way to save your life . . .

Brief pause.

I think we have to – indulge her.

ROBERTO. Indulge her?

GERARDO. Humour her, placate her, so she feels that we – that you, are willing to co-operate . . .

ROBERTO. I don't see how I can co-operate, given my rather peculiar position . . .

GERARDO. Indulge her, make her believe that you . . .

ROBERTO. Make her believe that I . . .

GERARDO. She promised me that if you – confessed she would be ready to –

ROBERTO. I haven't got anything to confess!

GERARDO. I think you're going to have to invent something then, because the only way she'll pardon you is if –

ROBERTO (*raises his voice, indignant*). She's got nothing to pardon me for. I did nothing and there's nothing to confess. Do you understand?

Upon hearing ROBERTO*'s voice,* PAULINA *gets up from her seat on the terrace and starts to move toward them.*

Instead of proposing dishonourable solutions to me, you should be out there convincing that madwoman of yours to cease this criminal behaviour before she ruins your career and ends up in jail or in an insane asylum. Tell her that. Or can't you impose a little order in your own house?

GERARDO. Roberto, I –

PAULINA *enters from the terrace.*

PAULINA. Any trouble, darling?

GERARDO. No trouble.

PAULINA. I just saw you a bit . . . agitated.

Brief pause.

Well, I see you've both finished your soup. No one can say I'm not a good cook, can they? Not an ideal housewife? Maybe this ideal housewife should serve you a teensy-weensy cup of coffee, Doctor? Though I believe the doctor here does not drink coffee. Doctor, I am speaking to you. Didn't your mother ever teach you that when –

ROBERTO. Leave my mother out of this. I forbid you to mention my mother.

Brief pause.

PAULINA. I'm sorry to have to agree with you. You're absolutely right. Your mother is not responsible for what you do. I don't know why men always insist on attacking mothers instead of – Why do they always say son of a bitch, why the bitch instead of the father who taught them in the first place to –

GERARDO. Paulina, would you please do me the favour of leaving so we can continue our conversation? Would you please do me that favour?

PAULINA. That favour and many more. I'll leave you men to fix the world.

She leaves and turns.

Oh, and if he wants to piss, darling, just snap your fingers and I'll come running.

She returns to the same spot on the terrace, watching.

ROBERTO. She's absolutely insane.

GERARDO. When crazy people have power, you've got to indulge them. In her case, a confession –

ROBERTO. But what could a confession – ?

GERARDO. Maybe it liberates her from her phantoms, how can I know what goes on in people's heads after they've been – but I think I understand that need of hers because it coincides with what we were talking about last night, the whole country's need to put into words what happened to us.

ROBERTO. And you?

GERARDO. What about me?

ROBERTO. You. What are you going to do afterwards?

GERARDO. After what?

ROBERTO. You believe her, don't you?

GERARDO. If I thought you were guilty, would I be trying so desperately to save your –

ROBERTO. From the beginning you've been conspiring with her. She plays the bad guy and you play the good guy and –

GERARDO. What do you mean by good –

ROBERTO. Playing roles, she's bad, you're good, to see if you can get me to confess that way. And once I've confessed, you're the one, not her, you're the one who's going to kill me, it's what any man would do, any real man, if they'd raped his wife, it's what I would do if somebody had raped my wife. Cut your balls off. So tell me: you think I'm that fucking doctor, don't you?

Pause. GERARDO *stands up.*

Where are you going?

GERARDO. I'm going to get the gun and blow your fucking brains out. (*Brief pause. Angrier and angrier.*) But first you sonuvabitch I'm going to follow your advice and cut off your balls, you fascist. That's what a real man does, doesn't he. Real macho men blow people's brains out and fuck women when they're tied up on cots. Not like me. I'm a stupid, yellow, soft faggot because I defend the son of a bitch who screwed my wife and destroyed her life. How many times did you screw her? How many times, you bastard?

ROBERTO. Gerardo, I . . . −

GERARDO. Gerardo is gone. I'm here. Me. An eye for an eye is here, a tooth for a tooth, right, isn't that our philosophy?

ROBERTO. I was only joking, it was a −

GERARDO. But on second thoughts, why should I dirty my hands with scum like you −

ROBERTO. − only a joke.

GERARDO. − when there's somebody who'll take much more pleasure in your pain and your death? Why take that one pleasure away from her? I'll call her right away so she can blow your fucking brains out herself.

ROBERTO. Don't go. Don't call her.

GERARDO. I'm tired of being in the middle, in between the two of you. You reach an understanding with her, you convince her.

ROBERTO. Gerardo, I'm scared.

Brief pause. GERARDO turns around, changes his tone.

GERARDO. So am I.

ROBERTO. Don't let her kill me.

Brief pause.

What are you going to say to her?

GERARDO. The truth. That you don't want to co-operate.

ROBERTO. I need to know what it is I did, you've got to

understand that I don't know what I have to confess. If
I were that man, I'd know every – detail, but I don't know
anything, right, so . . . if I make a mistake, she'll think
I'm – I'll need your help, you'd have to tell me so I can –
invent, invent, based on what you tell me.

GERARDO. You're asking me to deceive my wife?

ROBERTO. I'm asking you to save the life of an innocent
man, Escobar. You do believe that I'm innocent, don't you?

GERARDO. You care that much what I believe?

ROBERTO. Of course I do. She isn't the voice of civilisation,
you are. She isn't a member of the president's Commission,
you are.

GERARDO (*bitter, sad*). No, she isn't . . . Who gives a fuck
what she thinks. She's just . . .

He starts to leave.

ROBERTO. Wait. Where are you going? What are you going
to say to her?

GERARDO. I'm going to tell her that you need to piss.

Lights go down.

End of Act Two.

ACT THREE

Scene One

Just before evening. PAULINA *and* GERARDO *are outside, on the terrace facing the sea.* ROBERTO *inside, still tied up.* GERARDO *has the cassette recorder on his lap.*

PAULINA. I don't understand why.

GERARDO. I have to know.

PAULINA. Why?

Brief pause.

GERARDO. Paulina, I love you. I need to hear it from your lips. It's not fair that after so many years the person to tell me, ends up being him. It would be – intolerable.

PAULINA. Whereas if I tell you it would be – tolerable.

GERARDO. More tolerable than if he tells me first.

PAULINA. I told this to you already, Gerardo. Wasn't that enough?

GERARDO. Fifteen years ago you started to tell me and then . . .

PAULINA. Did you expect me to keep on talking to you with that bitch there? That bitch came out of your bedroom half naked asking why you were taking so long, and you expected me to –

GERARDO. She wasn't a bitch.

PAULINA. Did she know where I was? Of course she did. A bitch. Fuck a man whose woman wasn't exactly able to defend herself, huh?

GERARDO. We're not going to start all this again, Paulina.

PAULINA. You're the one who started.

GERARDO. How many times do I have to . . . ? – I'd spent two months trying to find you. Then she came by, she said she could help. We had a couple of drinks. My God, I'm also human.

PAULINA. While I defended your life, while your name stayed inside me and never left my mouth – Ask him, ask Miranda if I ever so much as whispered your name, while you . . .

GERARDO. You already forgave me, you forgave me, how many times will we have to go over this? We'll die from so much past, so much pain and resentment. Let's finish it – let's finish that conversation from years ago, let's close this book once and for all and never speak about it again, never again, never never again.

PAULINA. Forgive and forget, eh?

GERARDO. Forgive yes, forget, no. But forgive so we can start again. There's so much to live for, my . . .

PAULINA. What did you want me to do, to talk in front of her? To tell you, what they did to me, in front of her, that I should – ? How many times?

GERARDO. How many times what?

PAULINA. How many times did you fuck her?

GERARDO. Paulina . . .

PAULINA. How many?

GERARDO. Baby . . .

PAULINA. How many times did you do it? How many, how many? I tell you, you tell me.

GERARDO (*desperate, shaking her and then taking her in his arms*). Paulina, Paulina. You want to destroy me? Is that what you want?

PAULINA. No.

GERARDO. Well, you're going to destroy me. You're going to end up in a world where I don't exist, where I won't be here. Is that what you want?

PAULINA. I want to know how many times you fucked that bitch.

GERARDO. Don't do this to me, Paulina.

PAULINA. That wasn't the first night, was it, Gerardo? You'd seen her before, right? The truth, Gerardo.

GERARDO. People can die from an excessive dose of the truth, you know.

PAULINA. How many times, Gerardo. You tell me, I tell you.

GERARDO. Twice.

PAULINA. That night. What about before that night?

GERARDO (*very low*). Three times.

PAULINA. What?

GERARDO (*raising his voice*). Three times.

PAULINA. She was that good? You liked her that much? And she liked it too. She must have really enjoyed it if she came back for –

GERARDO. Do you understand what you're doing to me?

PAULINA. Beyond repair, huh? Irreparable.

GERARDO (*desperate*). What more do you want from me? We survived the dictatorship, we survived, and now we're going to do to each other what those bastards out there couldn't do to us? You want that?

PAULINA (*quietly*). No.

GERARDO. You want me to leave? Is that what you want? You want me to go out that door and never see you again? Good God, is that what you want?

PAULINA. No.

GERARDO. That's what you're going to get.

Brief pause.

I'm in your hands like a baby, I've got no defences, I'm naked in front of you like the day I was born. You want to treat me like you treat the man who –

PAULINA. No.

GERARDO. You want me to . . . ?

PAULINA (*murmuring*). I want you. You. I want you inside me, alive. I want you making love to me without ghosts in bed and I want you on the Commission defending the truth and I want you in the air I breathe and I want you in my Schubert that I can start listening to again –

GERARDO. Yes, Paulina, yes, yes.

PAULINA. – and I want us adopting a child and I want to care for you minute by minute like you took care of me after that night –

GERARDO. Never mention that bitch of a night again. If you go on and on about that night, you'll – kill me. Is that what you want?

PAULINA. No.

GERARDO. Are you going to tell me then?

PAULINA. Yes.

GERARDO. Everything?

PAULINA. Everything.

GERARDO. That's the way, that's how we'll get out of this mess – without hiding a thing from each other, together.

PAULINA. That's the way.

GERARDO. I'm going to turn on the recorder. You don't mind, love, if I turn it on?

PAULINA. Turn it on.

GERARDO *turns it on.*

GERARDO. Just as if you were sitting in front of the Commission.

PAULINA. I don't know how to begin.

GERARDO. Begin with your name.

PAULINA. My maiden name is Paulina Salas. Now I am married to Gerardo Escobar, the lawyer, but at that time –

GERARDO. Date.

PAULINA. April 6th, 1975, I was single. I was walking along San Antonio Street –

GERARDO. Be as precise as you can.

PAULINA. – at about two-fifteen in the afternoon, and when
I reached the corner at Huérfanos Street behind me I heard –
three men got out of a car, one of them stuck a gun in my
back, 'One word and we'll blow you away, Miss.' He spat
the words into my ear – he had garlic on his breath. I was
surprised that I should focus on such an insignificant detail,
the lunch he had eaten, begin to think about how he was
digesting that food with all the organs that I had been
studying in anatomy class. Later on I'd reproach myself,
I would have lots of time to think about it, why didn't
I call out, I knew that if that happened you're supposed to
scream, so people can know who is – call out your name,
I'm Paulina Salas, they're kidnapping me, if you don't
scream out that first moment you're already defeated, and
I submitted too easily, obeyed them right away without even
a gesture of defiance. All my life, I've always been much
too obedient.

The lights begin to go down.

The doctor wasn't among them. I met Doctor Miranda for
the first time three days later when . . . That's when I met
Doctor Miranda.

The lights go down further and PAULINA's *voice continues
in the darkness, only the cassette recorder lit by the light of
the moon.*

At first, I thought he would save me. He was so soft, so –
nice, after what the others had done to me. And then, all of
a sudden, I heard a Schubert quartet. There is no way of
describing what it means to hear that wonderful music in
the darkness, when you haven't eaten for the last three days,
when your body is falling apart, when . . .

In the darkness, we hear ROBERTO's *voice overlapping
with* PAULINA's *and the second movement of* Death and
the Maiden.

ROBERTO'S VOICE. I would put on the music because it
helped me in my role, the role of good guy, as they call it,
I would put on Schubert because it was a way of gaining the

prisoners' trust. But I also knew it was a way of alleviating
their suffering. You've got to believe it was a way of
alleviating the prisoners' suffering. Not only the music,
but everything else I did. That's how they approached me,
at first.

*The lights go up as if the moon were coming out. It is night-
time.* ROBERTO *is in front of the cassette recorder,
confessing. The Schubert fades.*

The prisoners were dying on them, they told me, they
needed someone to help care for them, someone they could
trust. I've got a brother, who was a member of the secret
services. You can pay the communists back for what they
did to Dad, he told me one night – my father had a heart
attack the day the peasants took over his land at Las
Toltecas. The stroke paralysed him – he lost his capacity for
speech, would spend hours simply looking at me, his eyes
said, Do something. But that's not why I accepted. The real
real truth, it was for humanitarian reasons. We're at war,
I thought, they want to kill me and my family, they want to
install a totalitarian dictatorship, but even so, they still have
the right to some form of medical attention. It was slowly,
almost without realising how, that I became involved in
more delicate operations, they let me sit in on sessions
where my role was to determine if the prisoners could
take that much torture, that much electric current. At first
I told myself that it was a way of saving people's lives, and
I did, because many times I told them – without it being
true, simply to help the person who was being tortured –
I ordered them to stop or the prisoner would die. But
afterwards I began to – bit by bit, the virtue I was feeling
turned into excitement – the mask of virtue fell off it and it,
the excitement, it hid, it hid, it hid from me what I was
doing, the swamp of what – By the time Paulina Salas was
brought in it was already too late. Too late.

The lights start to slowly go down.

ROBERTO. . . . too late. A kind of – brutalisation took over
my life, I began to really truly like what I was doing. It
became a game. My curiosity was partly morbid, partly

scientific. How much can this woman take? More than the other one? How's her sex? Does her sex dry up when you put the current through her? Can she have an orgasm under those circumstances? She is entirely in your power, you can carry out all your fantasies, you can do what you want with her.

The lights continue to fade while ROBERTO*'s voice speaks on in the semi-darkness, a beam of moonlight on the cassette recorder.*

Everything they have forbidden you since ever, whatever your mother ever urgently whispered you were never to do. You begin to dream with her, with all those women. Come on, Doctor, they would say to me, you're not going to refuse free meat, are you, one of them would sort of taunt me. His name was – they called him Stud – a nickname, because I never found out his real name. They like it, Doctor, Stud would say to me – all these bitches like it and if you put on that sweet little music of yours, they'll get even cosier. He would say this in front of the women, in front of Paulina Salas he would say it, and finally I, finally I – but not one ever died on me, not one of the women, not one of the men.

The lights go up and it is now dawning. ROBERTO, *untied, writes on a sheet of paper his own words from the cassette recorder. In front of him, many sheets of handwritten pages.* PAULINA *and* GERARDO *watch him.*

ROBERTO'S VOICE (*from the recorder*). As far as I can remember, I took part in the – interrogation of ninety-four prisoners, including Paulina Salas. It is all I can say. I ask forgiveness.

GERARDO *switches off the cassette recorder while* ROBERTO *writes.*

ROBERTO. – forgiveness.

GERARDO *switches the cassette recorder back on.*

ROBERTO'S VOICE. And I hope that this confession proves that I feel real repentance and that just as the country is reaching reconciliation and peace . . .

GERARDO *switches off the cassette recorder.*

GERARDO. Did you write that? Just as the country is reaching reconciliation and peace?

He switches it on again.

ROBERTO'S VOICE. – so too should I be allowed to live the rest of my days with my terrible secret. There can be no worse punishment than that which is imposed upon me by the voice of my conscience.

ROBERTO (*while he writes*). – punishment . . . my conscience.

GERARDO *switches off the cassette recorder. A moment's silence.*

And now what? You want me to sign?

PAULINA. First write there that this is all done of your own free will, without any sort of pressure whatsoever.

ROBERTO. That's not true.

PAULINA. You want real pressure, Doctor?

ROBERTO *writes down a couple of phrases, shows them to* GERARDO, *who moves his head affirmatively.* ROBERTO *signs.* PAULINA *looks at the signature, collects the paper, takes the cassette out of the recorder, puts another cassette in, pushes a button. We hear* ROBERTO's *confession on the tape.*

ROBERTO'S VOICE (*on tape*). I would put on the music because it helped me in my role, the role of good guy, as they call it, I would put on Schubert because it was a way of gaining the prisoners' trust. But I also knew it was a way of alleviating their suffering.

GERARDO. Paulina. It's over.

ROBERTO'S VOICE (*on tape*). You've got to believe it was a way of alleviating the prisoners' suffering.

GERARDO (*turning off the cassette recorder*). It is over.

PAULINA. Almost over, yes.

GERARDO. So don't you think it's about time we . . .

PAULINA. Right. We had an agreement.

She stands up, goes to the window, breathes in the air of the sea deeply.

To think that I would spend hours here like this, at dawn, trying to make out the things left behind by the tide during the night, staring at those shapes, wondering what they were, if they would be dragged out to sea again. And now . . . And now . . .

GERARDO. Paulina!

PAULINA (*turning suddenly*). I'm glad to see that you're still a man of principle. I thought I'd have to convince you now, now that you know he really is guilty, I thought I'd have to convince you not to kill him.

GERARDO. I wouldn't stain my soul with someone like him.

PAULINA (*throws him the keys to the car*). Right. Go and get his car.

Brief pause.

GERARDO. And I can leave him alone with you?

PAULINA. Wouldn't you say I'm old enough?

Brief pause.

GERARDO. All right, all right, I'll go get the car . . . Take care of yourself.

PAULINA. You too.

GERARDO *goes toward the door.*

PAULINA. Oh – and don't forget to give his jack back.

GERARDO (*trying to smile*). And don't you forget to return his Schubert cassette. You've got your own.

He exits. PAULINA *watches him leave.* ROBERTO *unties his ankles.*

ROBERTO. If you wouldn't mind, I would like to go to the bathroom. I suppose there is no reason why you should continue to accompany me?

PAULINA. Don't move, Doctor. There's still a little matter pending.

Brief pause.

It's going to be an incredibly beautiful day. You know the
only thing that's missing now, Doctor, the one thing I need
to make this day really truly perfect?

Brief pause .

To kill you. So I can listen to my Schubert without thinking
that you'll also be listening to it, soiling my day and my
Schubert and my country and my husband. That's what
I need . . .

ROBERTO. Madam, your husband left here trusting that you –
you gave your word . . .

PAULINA. But when I gave my word – I still had a doubt – a
teensy-weensy doubt – that you really were that man.
Because Gerardo was right, in his way. Proof, hard proof –
well, I could have been mistaken. But I knew that if you
confessed – and when I heard you, my last doubts vanished.
Now that I know, now that you are that man, I could not live
in peace with myself and let you live.

She points the gun at him.

You have a minute to pray, Doctor.

ROBERTO *slowly stands.*

ROBERTO. Don't do it. I'm innocent.

PAULINA. You've confessed.

ROBERTO. That confession, ma'am . . . It's false.

PAULINA. What do you mean, false?

ROBERTO. I made it up. We made it up.

PAULINA. It seemed quite true to me, painfully familiar as far
as I'm concerned . . .

ROBERTO. Your husband told me what to write, I invented
some of it, some of it was invented by me, but most of it
was what he got from you, from what he knew had
happened to you, so you'd let me go, he convinced me that
it was the only way that you wouldn't kill me and I had to –
you must know how, under pressure, we say anything, but
I'm innocent, Mrs. Escobar, God in Heaven knows that –

PAULINA. Do not invoke God, Doctor, when you are so close to finding out whether He exists or not. Stud.

ROBERTO. What?

PAULINA. Several times in your confession you mention Stud. He must have been a large man, muscular, he bit his fingernails, right, he bit his goddamn fingernails. Stud.

ROBERTO. I never met anyone like the man you're describing. The name was given to me by your husband. Everything I said comes from what your husband helped me to invent. Ask him when he comes back.

PAULINA. I don't need to ask him. I knew that he'd do that, I knew he'd use my words for your confession. That's the sort of person he is. He always thinks that he's more intelligent than everybody else, he always thinks that he's got to save somebody. I don't blame him. That's why I love him. We lied to each other out of love. He deceived me for my own good. I deceived him for his own good. But I'm the one who came out on top in this game. I gave him the name Bud, Doctor, I gave him the wrong name, to see if you would correct it. And you did correct it. You corrected the name Bud and you substituted the name Stud and if you were innocent –

ROBERTO. I'm telling you it was your husband who – Listen. Please listen. He must have thought Stud was the name a man like that would – I don't know why he – Ask him. Ask him.

PAULINA. It's not the only correction that you made. There were other. . . lies.

ROBERTO. What lies, what lies?

PAULINA. – small lies, small variations, that I inserted in my story to Gerardo, and you corrected most of them. It turned out just as I planned. You were so scared that if you didn't get it right . . . But I'm not going to kill you because you're guilty, Doctor, but because you haven't repented at all. I can only forgive someone who really repents, who stands up amongst those he has wronged and says, I did this, I did it, and I'll never do it again.

ROBERTO. What more do you want? You've got more than all the victims in this country will ever get.

He gets down on his knees.

What more do you want?

PAULINA. The truth, Doctor. The truth and I'll let you go. Repent and I'll let you go. You have ten seconds. One, two, three, four, five, six. Time is running out. Seven. Say it!

ROBERTO *stands up.*

ROBERTO. No. I won't. Because even if I confess, you'll never be satisfied. You're going to kill me anyway. So go ahead and kill me. I'm not going to let any sick woman treat me like this. If you want to kill me, do it. But you're killing an innocent man.

PAULINA. Eight.

ROBERTO. So someone did terrible things to you and now you're doing something terrible to me and tomorrow somebody else is going to – on and on and on. I have children, two boys, a girl. Are they supposed to spend the next fifteen years looking for you until they find you? And then –

PAULINA. Nine.

ROBERTO. Oh Paulina – isn't it time we stopped?

PAULINA. And why does it always have to be people like me who have to sacrifice, why are we always the ones who have to make concessions when something has to be conceded, why always me who has to bite her tongue, why? Well, not this time. This time I am going to think about myself, about what I need. If only to do justice in one case, just one. What do we lose? What do we lose by killing one of them? What do we lose? What do we lose?

They freeze in their positions as the lights begin to go down slowly. We begin to hear music from the last movement of Mozart's Dissonant Quartet. PAULINA *and* ROBERTO *are covered from view by a giant mirror which descends, forcing the members of the audience to look at themselves.*

For a few minutes, the Mozart quartet is heard, while the spectators watch themselves in the mirror. Selected slowly moving spots flicker over the audience, picking out two or three at a time, up and down rows.

Scene Two

A concert hall. An evening some months later. GERARDO and PAULINA appear, elegantly dressed. They sit down facing the mirror, their backs to the spectators, perhaps in two chairs or in two of the seats in the audience itself. Under the music we can hear typical sounds of an audience during a concert: throats clearing, an occasional cough, the ruffling of programme notes, even some heavy breathing. When the music ends, GERARDO begins to applaud and we can hear the applause growing from what is an invisible public. PAULINA does not applaud. The applause begins to die down and then we hear the habitual sounds that come from a concert hall when the first part of a programme is over: more throat clearing, murmurs, bodies shuffling toward the foyer. They both begin to go out, greeting people, stopping to chat for an instant. They slowly distance themselves from their seats and advance along an imaginary foyer which is apparently full of spectators. We hear mutterings, etc. GERARDO begins to talk to members of the audience, as if they were at the concert. His words can be heard above the murmurs of the public.

GERARDO (*intimately, talking to diverse spectators*). Why, thank you, thank you so much . . . Well, I am a bit tired, but it was worth it . . . Yes, we're very pleased with the Final Report of the Commission.

> PAULINA *slowly leaves him, going to one side where a small bar has been installed. GERARDO continues speaking with his audience until she returns.*

People are acting with enormous generosity, without the hint of seeking a personal vendetta . . . Well, I always knew that our work would help in the process of healing, but I was surprised it would start on the very first day we

convened. An old woman came in to testify. The woman
was so timid. She began to speak standing up. 'Please sit
down,' the president of the Commission said and stood up
to hold her chair for her. She sat down and began to sob.
Then she looked at us and said: 'This is the first time, sir,'
she said to us – her husband had disappeared fourteen years
ago, and she had spent thousands of hours petitioning,
thousands of hours waiting – 'This is the first time,' she
said to us, 'in all these years, sir, that somebody asks me to
sit down.' It was the first time that anyone had ever asked
her to sit down.

Meanwhile, PAULINA *has bought some candy – and as she
pays,* ROBERTO *enters, under a light which has a faint
phantasmagoric moonlight quality. He could be real or he
could be an illusion in* PAULINA*'s head.* PAULINA *does
not see him yet. A bell goes off to indicate that the concert
is about to recommence. She returns to* GERARDO*'s side
who, by this time, should be finishing his monologue.*
ROBERTO *stays behind, watching* PAULINA *and*
GERARDO *from a distance.*

As for the murderers, even if we do not know or cannot
reveal their names – ah, Paulie, just in time. Well, I'll see
you later, old man. Now I've finally got some free time.
Maybe we could have a couple of drinks at home. Pau
mixes a margarita that'll stand your hair on end.

GERARDO *and* PAULINA *sit in their seats.* ROBERTO
goes to another seat, always looking at PAULINA.
*Applause is heard when the imaginary musicians come on.
The instruments are tested and tuned. Then* Death and the
Maiden *begins.* GERARDO *looks at* PAULINA, *who looks
forward. He takes her hand and then also begins to look
forward. After a few instants, she turns slowly and looks at*
ROBERTO. *Their eyes interlock for a moment. Then she
turns her head and faces the stage and the mirror. The
lights go down while the music plays and plays and plays.*

Curtain .

Afterword to the Original Stage Play

Eight or nine years ago, when General Augusto Pinochet was still the dictator of Chile and I was still in exile, I began tentatively exploring in my mind a dramatic situation that was someday to become the core of *Death and the Maiden*. A man whose car breaks down on the highway is given a lift home by a friendly stranger. The man's wife, believing she recognises in the stranger the voice of the torturer who raped her some years before, kidnaps him and decides to put him on trial. On several occasions I sat down to scribble what I then imagined would be a novel. A few hours and a couple of unsatisfactory pages later, I would give up in frustration. Something essential was missing. I could not figure out, for instance, who the woman's husband was, how he would react to her violence, if he would believe her. Nor were the historical circumstances under which the story developed clear to me, the symbolic and secret connections to the larger life of the country itself, the world beyond the narrow, claustrophobic boundaries of that woman's home. The use of a forceps may be necessary to ensure the birth of a child that needs help out of the womb, but I had by then blessedly learned that when characters do not want to be born, forceps may scar them and twist their lives irreparably. My trio would, unfortunately, have to wait.

They were forced to wait a long time. It was not until Chile returned to democracy in 1990 and I myself therefore returned to resettle there with my family after seventeen years of exile, that I finally understood how the story had to be told.

My country was at the time (and still is now as I write this) living an uneasy transition to democracy, with Pinochet no longer the president but still in command of the armed forces, still able to threaten another coup if people became unruly or, more specifically, if attempts were made to punish the human rights violations of the outgoing regime. And in order to avoid chaos and constant confrontation, the new government had to find a way of not alienating Pinochet supporters who continued occupying significant areas of power in the judiciary, the senate, the town councils – and particularly the economy. In the area of human rights, our democratically elected president, Patricio Aylwin, responded to this quandary by naming a Commission – called the Rettig Commission, after the eighty-year-old lawyer who headed it – that would investigate the crimes of the dictatorship that had ended in death or its presumption, but which would neither name the perpetrators nor judge them. This was an important step toward healing a sick country: the truth of the terror unleashed upon us that we had always known in a private and fragmented fashion would finally receive public recognition, established forever as official history, recreating a community fractured by divisions and hatred that we wished to leave behind. On the other hand, justice would not be done and the traumatic experience of hundreds of thousands of other victims, those who had survived, would not even be addressed. Aylwin was steering a prudent but valiant course between those who wanted past terror totally buried and those who wanted it totally revealed.

As I watched with fascination how the Commission carried out its difficult task, it slowly dawned on me that here might be the key to the unresolved story that had been buzzing inside my head for so many years: that fictitious kidnapping and trial should occur, not in a nation under the boot of a dictator, but in one that was in transition to democracy, where so many Chileans were grappling with the hidden traumas of what had been done to them while other Chileans wondered if their crimes would now be revealed. It also became clear that the way to make the husband of the tortured woman have a tremendous stake in the outcome of that kidnapping was to make him a member of a commission similar to the one headed by Rettig. And it did not take me long to conclude that, rather than a novel, what needed to be written was a play.

It was a risky idea. I knew from experience that distance is often the best ally of an author and that when we deal with events that are being enacted and multiplied in immediate history, a danger always exists of succumbing to a 'documentary' or overly realistic approach, losing universality and creative freedom, trying to adjust the characters to the events unfolding around us rather than letting them emerge on their own, letting them surprise and disturb us. I also knew that I would be savagely criticised by some in my own country for 'rocking the boat' by reminding everyone about the long-term effects of terror and violence on people precisely at a time when we were being asked to be notably cautious.

I felt, however, that if as a citizen I had to be responsible and reasonable, as an artist I had to answer the wild mating call of my characters and break the silence which was weighing upon so many of my self-censored compatriots, fearful of creating 'trouble' for the new democracy. It was then and is now more than ever my belief that a fragile democracy is strengthened by expressing for all to see the deep dramas and sorrows and hopes that underlie its existence and that it is not by hiding the damage we have inflicted on ourselves that we will avoid its repetition.

As I began to write I found the characters trying to figure out the sort of questions that so many Chileans were asking themselves privately, but that hardly anyone seemed interested in posing in public. How can those who tortured and those who were tortured co-exist in the same land? How to heal a country that has been traumatised by repression if the fear to speak out is still omnipresent everywhere? And how do you reach the truth if lying has become a habit? How do we keep the past alive without becoming its prisoner? How do we forget it without risking its repetition in the future? Is it legitimate to sacrifice the truth to ensure peace? And what are the consequences of suppressing that past and the truth it is whispering or howling to us? Are people free to search for justice and equality if the threat of a military intervention haunts them? And given these circumstances, can violence be avoided? And how guilty are we all of what happened to those who suffered most? And perhaps the greatest dilemma of them all: how to confront these issues without destroying the national consensus, which creates democratic stability?

Three weeks later, *Death and the Maiden* was ready.

If the play revealed many of the hidden conflicts that were just under the surface of the nation, and therefore posed a clear threat to people's psychological security, it could also be an instrument through which we explored our identity and the contradictory options available to us in the years to come.

A multitude of messages of the contemporary imagination, specifically those that are channelled through the mass entertainment media, assure us, over and over, that there is an easy, even facile, comforting, answer to most of our problems. Such an aesthetic strategy seems to me not only to falsify and disdain human experience but in the case of Chile or of any country that is coming out of a period of enormous conflict and pain, it turns out to be counterproductive for the community, freezing its maturity and growth. I felt that *Death and the Maiden* touched upon a tragedy in an almost Aristotelian sense, a work of art that might help a collective to purge itself, through pity and terror, in other words to force the spectators to confront those predicaments that, if not brought into the light of day, could lead to their ruin.

Which is a way of stating that this piece of fiction, as so much of what I had written previously in my novels, stories, poems, and other plays, was not merely Chilean in scope but addressed problems that could be found all over the world, all over the twentieth century, all over the face of humanity through the ages. It was not only about a country that is afraid and simultaneously needful of understanding its fear and its scars, not only about the long-term effects of torture and violence on human beings and the beautiful body of their land, but about other themes that have always obsessed me: what happens when women take power. How can you tell the truth if the mask you have adopted ends up being identical to your face? How does memory beguile and save and guide us? How can we keep our innocence once we have tasted evil? How to forgive those who have hurt us irreparably? How do we find a language that is political but not pamphletary? How to tell stories that are both popular and ambiguous, stories that can be understood by large audiences and yet contain stylistic experimentation, that are mythical and also about immediate human beings?

Death and the Maiden appears in English at a moment when humanity is undergoing extraordinary changes, when there is great hope for the future and great confusion about what that future may bring. In the current debate, little is being heard from that submerged zone of our species who live far from the centres of power but are often near the quick centre of suffering where ethical choices determine the immediate shape of things to come and things to be postponed. In times such as these, when the more miserable and distant lands seem to disappear from the horizon, it may help us a bit, perhaps a teensy-weensy bit, I would hope, to think of the Paulinas, the Gerardos, the Robertos, of the world – to figure out for ourselves which of these three we most resemble, how much of our secluded lives are expressed in each of these characters and in all of them. Until finally, I would also hope, we would realise that what we feel when we watch and whisper and ache with these faraway people from faraway Chile could well be that strange trembling state of humanity we call recognition, a bridge across our divided globe.

Ariel Dorfman, 11 September 1991

READER

for

Rodrigo and Joaquín

with thanks for their company and their existence

Characters

DANIEL LUCAS, *around fifty years old. Could be older.*
  Or a bit younger. The same actor plays
DON ALFONSO MORALES

IRENE, *a secretary, in her thirties. The same actress plays*
JACQUELINE.

NICK (NICHOLAS) LUCAS, *Daniel Lucas's son,*
  around twenty-five/thirty. The same actor plays
ENRIQUE MORALES *and*
DAVID MALKO, *a writer.*

DIRECTOR, *around Daniel Lucas's age. Could be a bit older*
  or a bit younger.

TANYA, *a shadow woman, Daniel Lucas's former wife,*
  between twenty and thirty years old. The same actress plays
SONIA, *David Malko's wife.*

MAN, *ageless. Can only play himself.*

Time: the near future.

Place: everywhere.

The play can be staged without an intermission.

ACT ONE

Darkness.

A beam of light comes up on the MAN *on one side of the
stage. He makes a gesture and next to him a chair appears in
another beam of light. He examines the chair, measuring it
carefully, with some satisfaction. He makes another gesture
and the chair disappears, swallowed by the darkness and,
simultaneously, swirling, murky lights go up on an office.
We can vaguely see the figures of a man and a woman sitting
on either side of a desk, but we cannot hear what they are
saying. The* MAN *walks up to the lighted area, stops at its
edge, listens. Then he begins to measure the perimeter of the
office. He smiles. He makes another gesture and the light
grows and we begin to hear the man and the woman: he is*
DON ALFONSO MORALES *and the woman is his secretary,*
JACQUELINE. DON ALFONSO *is a man of some fifty years,
though he could be older – or younger: streaks of white in
his hair, prominent eyebrows, a suit with a stiff shirt and tie.*
JACQUELINE *is an extremely attractive, vivacious woman
in her thirties. The office furniture is very sparse: a desk (its
top could be held in place by two pillars of books), two chairs,
a window through which we can see verdant forests. Next to
the desk is an umbrella.*

DON ALFONSO. Next!

JACQUELINE. No subsidy at all, Don Alfonso? Not even one
peso?

DON ALFONSO. Nothing. No talent. You can't argue with
talent. You possess it or you don't. And this lady – no
matter what her other attributes –

JACQUELINE. But her husband knows the Minister of –

DON ALFONSO. I don't care what corrupt dealings her
spouse has with anybody! No favouritism here. The lady
has no talent. I will not allow a tree to expire to satisfy her

vanity. When I pronounce the word next, Jacqueline, that is exactly what I mean.

JACQUELINE (*looking inside a huge folder*). Alright, alright! 'Secret Gourmet Dishes from the Convent' by Sister Carolina.

DON ALFONSO. Now. In these monastic sauces, miss, there is no malice. No pollution, no aphrodisiacs, only natural herbs used. 200 copies recycled paper. Next?

The MAN *smiles, makes another gesture. Lights go down on him.*

JACQUELINE. 'Butcheries', a collection of poems by Lircay Santiago.

DON ALFONSO. Our salacious Lircay is in a bit of trouble. A thousand copies? What does he think we are – a paper factory?

JACQUELINE. You're forbidding him?

DON ALFONSO. Jacqueline: I detest the word forbid. We allocate scant resources, we set priorities, we make sure that the taxpayers are not subsidising smut. We never forbid.

JACQUELINE. Did you know that Lircay's wife is expecting their sixth child next month? Couldn't we allocate –

DON ALFONSO. Let nobody complain about my munificence.

JACQUELINE. Mugnificence?

DON ALFONSO. Cultivate your dictionary, my dear. Mu-ni-fi-cence. As for Lircay, tell him to put in an appearance – let's see, next Wednesday – so we can execute some editorial adjustments, a snip-snap here and there. But only a small grant.

JACQUELINE. What sort of adjustments?

DON ALFONSO. Take page 45, where it says – Oh if the moon could masturbate –

JACQUELINE (*taking notes*). – on page 45 where it says – does it really say that, Don Alfonso, on page 45?

DON ALFONSO. We could substitute: Oh if we might discern the uncertainty of sin in the waning moon.

JACQUELINE. Brilliant. You would have made one hell of a writer, I can tell you that.

DON ALFONSO *scratches the left side of his head with his right hand.*

DON ALFONSO. I am perfectly content with my present position, thank you. I had the writing fever when I was – I'll admit that, but now – what on earth would I be writing about now?

JACQUELINE. About you. And about . . . me. You. And me.

JACQUELINE *crosses to him, grabs his hand.* DON ALFONSO *quickly evades her, goes limping to the door of the office, opens it.*

DON ALFONSO. Miss, we have subscribed to a pact. I do not need to remind you that we are in a public place.

JACQUELINE (*going to door*). What is public can be transformed with the touch of a toe, darling (*She closes the door with her foot.*) into something extremely private. Today's Thursday.

JACQUELINE *takes one of his hands and puts it on her breast.*

So – what would you call this, Alfonso?

DON ALFONSO (*withdrawing his hand*). That is called a – bosom.

JACQUELINE (*whispering*). Tit, my love, it's a darling tit. (*Louder.*) Such an expert with words, my Alfonsito, and you never manage to call things by their names.

She kisses him. DON ALFONSO *responds passionately. He disengages, gently sits her down in the chair, begins to limp to the door, stops when he hears* JACQUELINE's *next words.*

JACQUELINE. I bet you said 'tit' to – her. I bet you wrote poems to her, back when you wanted to be a writer, before you took this . . .

DON ALFONSO. What I used to converse with my wife is my business.

JACQUELINE. How about that other woman?

DON ALFONSO *scratches the left side of his head with his right hand.*

DON ALFONSO. What other woman?

JACQUELINE. A woman who came to ask for you this morning. She – well, seemed to know intimate details about you. The sort of things women know when –

DON ALFONSO. When what?

JACQUELINE. When she's . . . made love to a man. (*Pause.*) Passionately. With nothing between them but the skin she was born with. And even that's about to melt. Melt magnificently. Look it up in the dictionary. Magnificently.

DON ALFONSO. Who was it? Who was the woman?

JACQUELINE. It was . . . It was . . . Nobody.

DON ALFONSO. What do you mean, nobody?

JACQUELINE. A joke, you silly. I made her up. To see how you –

DON ALFONSO. I am not fond of your jokes.

JACQUELINE. Just wanted to see if you were hiding something from me, darling.

DON ALFONSO. Don't you darling me.

JACQUELINE. Just wanted to see if you trusted me.

There is a pause. DON ALFONSO *limps to the door, opens it.*

JACQUELINE. Your silence is eloquent.

DON ALFONSO. Silence is never eloquent, woman. Let me say no more. We have wasted enough time. To work. Our mission for today and every day: Making a tree happy . . .

JACQUELINE. Without making a writer sad. That's the mission for today – what about tonight's mission? Thursday night?

DON ALFONSO. It is not my impression, miss, that it is night-time. In fact there are exactly three hours and forty-six minutes before the sun sets today.

JACQUELINE. Why you even know the time the sun sets each

day, Señor Morales. It's lucky for me that's not the only thing you know . . .

DON ALFONSO. It is lucky for you that I am – so fond of your idle prattle. Just remember: 'Power without . . . '

JACQUELINE. Yeah, yeah, responsibility. 'Power without responsibility, the prerogative of the harlot through the ages.' I've heard it a thousand times. Stanley, Earl Baldwin, must have invented it while he was – you know what he must have been doing . . . Probably doing it to his secretary – and she was thinking, you know what she was thinking, while old Baldwin was humping away?

DON ALFONSO. How could I possibly know what she was thinking?

JACQUELINE *cuddles up to* DON ALFONSO, *provocative and ironic.*

JACQUELINE. 'Responsibility without power, the fate of the secretary through the ages.' You can quote me on it.

ENRIQUE MORALES *enters. He is dressed extravagantly, has a brash, expansive manner, almost hyper.*

ENRIQUE. Mot-mot, pops. Jackie, my dear.

JACQUELINE *and* DON ALFONSO *separate, startled.*

ENRIQUE. I'm sure I'm not interrupting, as you did say you wanted to . . . . Urgent, you said. Five o'clock, you said.

DON ALFONSO. Yes, yes, of course. We've done our work for the day.

ENRIQUE. Are you sure? Saved enough trees? Made enough writers over-happy? What about this one?

ENRIQUE *goes to the desk, picks up a manuscript, opens it randomly towards the end.*

ENRIQUE. 'Coming Together.' Intriguing title.

DON ALFONSO. Put that down.

ENRIQUE. Oh you know I don't read. Not me. Not us, pops. We're into screens. Images? Mot, mot? Let's see. Maybe I've forgotten how to read. Not quite.

ENRIQUE *begins to read from the manuscript.*

ENRIQUE (*reading*). ' "Let me ask you something." The man's voice came from faraway, as if it were telegraphed instead of spoken. "Let me ask you something. If you had to choose between possessing a man's body and possessing his soul, what would you choose?" '

DON ALFONSO. I said to put that down.

ENRIQUE. Boring, boring! Just my luck. Possessing the soul? I was hoping for a steamy bedroom scene. I was hoping for naked bodies. Where've you got them stashed? Come on, confess.

DON ALFONSO. Stashed?

ENRIQUE. The hot stuff, pops. You must have it all stashed away somewhere. We could divide the plunder. Look, I'll front for you.

DON ALFONSO. What are you talking about?

ENRIQUE. Purple eyes! I'm talking about pesos for purple eyes. How'd I look up there, strumming a guitar with my scalpel, Dr. Enrique Morales and his Purple Eyes Banda? Courtesy of the anthology I'm planning – Howling virgins, depraved eunuchs, thrusting unicorns – My Anthology, pops, remember? Forbidden Latino Readings – Come on, pops, nobody would ever guess who was the real compiler of –

DON ALFONSO. You shouldn't even joke about these matters, Enrique. If the tree-police were to –

ENRIQUE. Who'd listen to me here? In the office of Mr. Loyalty?

But you're right – point taken, mot-mot. Life is the only joke, but some things in it – like what can be done to our bodies – are serious as the smile of hell.

Isn't that so, Jackie?

ENRIQUE *comes onto her.*

JACQUELINE. If you've finished with me, Don Alfonso . . . I've got some shopping to do for my mother. She hasn't been well lately.

DON ALFONSO *stands, limping slightly, and escorts her out.*

ENRIQUE. Hey, I can keep your Mama company, Jackie, I can do her shopping – and you can stay here with pops. One happy family.

DON ALFONSO. Please accept my apologies for my son's behaviour, miss.

JACQUELINE. Don Alfonso, you're the last gentleman left in the world.

JACQUELINE *exits angrily, closing the door.* ENRIQUE *immediately changes his attitude, becomes reserved, serious, intent.*

DON ALFONSO. That was outrageous.

ENRIQUE. It was expedient.

DON ALFONSO. That is no way to treat a lady.

ENRIQUE. Don't try to give me lessons about how men should treat women.

DON ALFONSO. Oh, so that's what we're here for today?

ENRIQUE. You asked me to come. You tell me.

DON ALFONSO. No. You tell me. About this!

DON ALFONSO *picks up the manuscript* ENRIQUE *had been reading from.*

DON ALFONSO. This preposterous futuristic novel. 'Coming Together.' Coming apart it should be – You insinuate yourself into this office with your sweet smiles, all charms, with the transparent subterfuge that one of your eternally unnamed friends wrote this trash, 'could I have your opinion, pops, could you authorise it for publication, mot-mot' – but I know who wrote it, I know who – and in fact, I don't know whether to be angrier because it's a bunch of irresponsible political claptrap and is going to land you and probably me in jail or if – what really hurts me, you want to know what really hurts me?

ENRIQUE. I didn't think anything could ever hurt you, Dad.

DON ALFONSO. What hurts me are the lies –

ENRIQUE. What lies?

A light comes up on the MAN. *He is standing behind the chair.* TANYA, *a young woman is seated in it, bound and gagged.*

DON ALFONSO. The lies about your mother. How dare you imply that she – and it's you, not your fictitious friend, don't even try to deny it – that she died in a Readjustment Centre – that I – just when my enemies are spreading stories, trying to ruin my – How dare you ask me, me of all people, to authorise this –

ENRIQUE. Prove me wrong.

A phone rings from the darkness. The MAN *takes the gag off* TANYA. *She looks towards* DON ALFONSO. *He doesn't see her.*

DON ALFONSO. What?

ENRIQUE. You say the stories aren't true? Prove me wrong. Publish this book. Go ahead. Release it. I'd love to be wrong.

DON ALFONSO. Well, you are wrong. And what I can't understand – My God, I know it hasn't been easy, I've tried to be a father and a – what I can't understand is how you could write this down and not even give me the chance to defend myself. Look. Look.

DON ALFONSO *shows his son the novel, begins to leaf through it. The phone rings again. Lights on* ENRIQUE *begin to slowly fade.*

ENRIQUE (*almost a shadow*). I have proof, Dad. And I'm the one who needs to understand. You sent her there, to die there, in that place. Just tell me why. Why did you do it? What were you so afraid of?

The phone is still ringing. ENRIQUE *has almost disappeared.*

TANYA. What were you so afraid of?

ENRIQUE'S VOICE. What were you so afraid of?

DON ALFONSO. Nothing. Nothing.

The phone rings one more time.

DON ALFONSO (*shouting*). Answer that Goddamned phone!

Lights disappear on MAN *and* TANYA. *Bright, cheerful LIGHTS rise on the office and the anteroom adjoined to it.* IRENE, *played by the same actress who plays* JACQUELINE, *answers the phone. We are in* DANIEL LUCAS'*s office in the Moral Resources Company in the future. All of a sudden, under a different light, everything seems more futuristic, the furniture and the desk high-tech. Through the window where we saw verdant luxury, there now pulse electronic, psychodelic images. The umbrella becomes a decoration.* DON ALFONSO *is transformed into* DANIEL LUCAS, *leaning against his desk, rigid. He scratches the right side of his head with his left hand.*

ENRIQUE'S VOICE. What were you so afraid of?

DANIEL LUCAS (*reading from the manuscript*). 'What were you so afraid of?' And Don Alfonso Morales answered his son with his favourite word of the last twenty years: 'Nothing.'' Nothing. Nothing, huh?

IRENE presses a button. An intercom buzzes. DANIEL LUCAS *ignores it, keeps reading.*

'All his latino life, Don Alfonso Morales had proclaimed that dreams are meaningless. Someday the species would overcome this annoying habit of the mind as it had successfully defeated the need to walk on all fours. And yet he had dreamt last night this very encounter with his son.'

Another buzz. DANIEL *answers the intercom.*

Is that you, Irene?

IRENE. Who did you expect, Mr. Lucas? Christopher Columbus?

DANIEL LUCAS. Your jokes get funnier every day, Irene. What is it?

IRENE. Your son Nick is on the way. Just as you asked, Mr. Lucas. And a publisher just called. Bergante. He wanted to know if you'd already read the manuscript by David Malko he –

DANIEL LUCAS. He must have psychic powers. I'm reading it now.

IRENE. So? What d'you think?

DANIEL LUCAS. It's a . . . – If that damn Bergante would cease interrupting me, I would by now have determined if we can green-light this project. Tell him that.

IRENE. Right. I'll tell him that.

DANIEL LUCAS. No – wait! About the author, this Malko person – ask Bergante . . . . his name.

IRENE. We know his name. David Malko.

DANIEL LUCAS. Well, I thought this Malko – he might be – you know, a pseudonym.

IRENE. I'll ask Bergante. Anything else?

DANIEL LUCAS. Could you – join me for a few minutes, there's something . . . there's something . . .

IRENE. Disturbing you?

DANIEL LUCAS. Yes.

    IRENE *enters, closing the door.*

DANIEL LUCAS. The door, the door. Miss, we have sub-scribed to a pact. I do not need to remind you that we are in – that we are in – I do not need –

IRENE. You do not need . . . ?

DANIEL LUCAS (*recomposing himself*). In fact, it's good you closed the door. For once, you have been foresightful. Because I – it's this damned manuscript that Bergante sent me to see if we could authorise an option, it's –

IRENE. 'Turns' by David Malko?

DANIEL LUCAS. I haven't finished it yet but –

IRENE. Well, Bergante says it doesn't have an ending yet. That's why he sent it to you, to see if you could suggest – some rewrites that would –

DANIEL LUCAS. I have no suggestions. Who cares how it ends? The author of this 'Turns' – ha! 'Returns' it should be called – the author is obviously one of those spoiled young

people who take pure bodies, pure thoughts, a pure planet
for granted without ever pondering the sacrifices we made
to get here. Take notes.

IRENE. Mr. Lucas . . .

DANIEL LUCAS. I'll use these thoughts for the speech I'm
giving at the BookSellers Association when they honour my
Twenty Years of Moral Service to Art. I'll tell them about
these youngsters who hardly know how to write anymore
and don't have memories of how things were before – when
the great plague was raging, violence and sex on every
screen – so the minor sacrifices and restrictions that seem
natural to older people look unnecessary to them. Are you
taking notes?

IRENE. Mr. Lucas. Are you sure we're talking about the same
book? Bergante says it happens a long time ago, in a small
impoverished Spanish-American country, he said – and
there's an ecofascist dictatorship, a terrible place according
to – And we've got democracy, so how can – ?

DANIEL LUCAS. Would you cease your cackling, woman?
This Malko fellow, he's a clever one – he's set it far away,
long ago, riding the ecological fad to snipe at us. Look –
he's breaking every guideline in sight. Twenty-second kisses
on screen. A hand on a – bosom. A man and a woman in the
same bed together. Let me say no more.

IRENE. Before, during or after?

DANIEL LUCAS. After. But that's not what – what –

IRENE. Disturbs you? We can fix the kisses. Cut them to the
regulatory two seconds.

DANIEL LUCAS. Stop defending the bastard. Look – in
this script there's a certain Don Alfonso Morales, he's a –
censor – in some sort of – it's some sort of Office or Library
or Ministry back then that controls the flow of books – an
absurd premise, though I have read that in certain poor
countries during the twentieth century paper was rationed
supposedly to save the forests – but of course it was merely
a sham for them to export all the trees while the thought
police controlled the – Listen, Irene, this pompous idiot of a

censor – his son Enrique – Enrique's a medical student
who's secretly written a book that irresponsibly accuses
the – but what matters is that this man's wife – the Morales
man, not his son, – it's the man's wife who really – and if
the son's suspicions – but of course the son's in danger –

IRENE. You've got to excuse me, Mr. Lucas, but you're really –
why, you're rambling!

DANIEL LUCAS. Listen to this. 'Don Alfonso Morales
scratched the left side of his head. And he scratched it, as
usual, with his right hand.' Well . . . ?

IRENE. Well, what?

DANIEL LUCAS. Doesn't this palely – remind you of
somebody?

DANIEL LUCAS *scratches the right side of his head with
his left hand.*

IRENE (*laughing*). You think that . . .

DANIEL LUCAS. Yes.

IRENE. You really think that somebody has . . . That this
Malko who you don't even know . . .

DANIEL LUCAS. Yes.

IRENE. You could be wrong. After all, you scratch your right
ear with your left hand, Daniel, so –

DANIEL LUCAS. No. The man – there are other parallels that –

IRENE. Well, congratulations, then. How does it feel, to be a
hero in –

DANIEL LUCAS. The man's not a hero. He's a – I don't want
that Alfonso Morales out there for anybody to see, my co-
facilitators would crucify me – Why, the man's – detestable.
He's a – a censor for a brutal tyranny. And he's – Latin-
American. And – he limps! The bastard is a cripple. In
body. And in mind. An unfeeling son of a bitch.

IRENE. Then he's got nothing to do with you – Your legs are
magnificently sturdy – and you should –

DANIEL LUCAS. Magnificently. Right. Except that in other
things –

IRENE. – so why should you . . . I mean, Nick's not in trouble, is he?

DANIEL LUCAS. Certainly not.

IRENE. So you're just imagining things. And maybe you should give the project a green light, so nobody can say you're prejudiced against something that seems so close to home, so to speak. Maybe if we suggest some rewrites and allow this Malko to resubmit. Because sponsors have been demanding more dramas with Latino themes – and if we can get a crippled actor to do the role of this Morales guy, then –

DANIEL LUCAS. No.

IRENE. How about a reading with Latino actors to see if – ?

DANIEL LUCAS. No.

IRENE. Not even conditionally denied production, so he – ?

DANIEL LUCAS. No, no, no. Nothing whatsoever.

Abruptly the DIRECTOR *enters out of nowhere.*

DIRECTOR. Is this music to my ears? Or disharmony? A stream of negatives. Interdictions. Denials. No, no, no. Nothing whatsoever. It's good to keep the standards and the practices high – but let's hope we're not keeping juicy cultural material from the viewers, Luke.

DANIEL LUCAS. We're here to serve the viewers, sir.

DIRECTOR. And the sponsors. Thirsting for the newest. So I should not interrupt –

DANIEL LUCAS. The Director of Moral Resources is always welcome in this office.

DIRECTOR. I'd better be. Because I've been protecting you, Luke. You're one lucky bastard. D' you know that? D'you know what your co-facilitators call you? (*Pause.*) What do they call you? (*Pause.*)

IRENE (*blurting it out*). The Pope.

DIRECTOR (*looks her over*). 'Cause he's infallible, right? 'Cause you're infallible, Danny Lucas. How long have we . . . ?

DANIEL LUCAS. Twenty years, sir.

DIRECTOR. Twenty years and you haven't made one mistake. That's a great nickname. (*Pause.*) Give me a hint, Luke, a hint, a clue, an inkling, tell me. You've authorised more scripts than anyone else in this building, anonymously bestowed more production slips, rewritten endings, doctored scenes, more than – Has one of the shows you originated ever been denounced as pornographic? Have the Supreme Justices of Preservation ever accused you of wasting our moral and bodily resources?

We hear a series of melodious chimes in the air. The DIRECTOR *immediately stops talking and turns to* DANIEL LUCAS, *gives him a hug, then hugs* IRENE, *then* IRENE *hugs* DANIEL, *then all three stand there smiling happily. The chimes continue for a few more beats, then die out. The three return to their former positions.*

DIRECTOR. Don't you just love the Smiley Minute? Makes you feel so – upbeat, so – But where was I?

IRENE . . . . wasting our moral and bodily resources . . .

DIRECTOR. Right, correct, absolutely. That's it. Has this Production Company ever been sued by a husband because one of our programmes induced his wife to adultery? And the ratings – have we ever lost one ratings sweep since you joined us? The Pope? Ha! That's what they used to call me. At about the time I discovered you. The Pope? Old Eagle Eyes, that's what they call you. How d' you do it, Luke? How in hell do you – ? What's the secret?

DANIEL LUCAS. There is no secret, Director. It's merely a matter of – culture, taste I suppose we could call it.

DIRECTOR. Show me.

DANIEL LUCAS. Show you what, sir?

DIRECTOR. How you do it. Take anything – this manuscript, for instance – 'Turns' – by David Malko . . . ?

DANIEL LUCAS. I think this one's not ready, not quite –

DIRECTOR. Better yet. Maybe we can give the writer some pointers.

DANIEL LUCAS. There are more stimulating texts than –

DIRECTOR (*ignoring him*). Take this dialogue. (*To* IRENE.)
Come here, my dear, and help me out. You'll do the woman
and I'll do the man – unless, of course, you'd like to reverse
positions?

IRENE. I'll do the woman.

DIRECTOR. By all means. Let me see now. Why, there's a
Director in this novel. Hey, maybe I could do a cameo-play
myself, you know.

DANIEL LUCAS. I don't think you would care to play that
role, sir. The man's a bit of – a villain.

DIRECTOR. Better to play the villain in a movie than to be a
villain in reality. Now, let's see: 'The Director watched the
face of a woman emerge from the shadows, as if from the
darkness of the dead.' Well, that's not a bad way of
beginning a scene. Suspense, huh, tension, apprehension.
Then this man, he says: 'You haven't aged,' that's what the
Director – 'Why, look at you, you're still a girl. What have
you been doing with yourself, to your little self, to stop
time?' Hmmm. Not quite original, to greet someone that
way, but – you can't always be snappy, I guess.

DANIEL LUCAS. It is meant as a metaphor, sir, I believe.
Ironically.

DIRECTOR. Why's that?

DANIEL LUCAS. The woman in question – she was thought
to be dead.

DIRECTOR. Dead?

DANIEL LUCAS. In a manner of speaking, sir. Interned for
life in a – one of these mental institutions.

DIRECTOR. Like one of our Readjustment Centres?

DANIEL LUCAS. Yes, sir. So to greet her in that way . . .

DIRECTOR. Aha! A metaphor! I see. This is getting
interesting. Now it's your turn, Irene. Here. 'I've been
waiting for my boy to grow up. So he can learn the truth.'

IRENE (*reading*). 'I've been waiting for my boy to grow up.
So he can learn the truth.'

DIRECTOR (*reading*). 'He'll never believe you. He adores his
   father.'

DANIEL LUCAS *watches the scene in great agitation.*

IRENE (*reading*). 'That's why I'm going to make his father
   tell him the truth.'

DIRECTOR (*reading*). 'You're crazy.'

IRENE (*reading*). 'Yes, I know. That's what the limping
   bastard said to me. And that Judge – when he stopped me
   from seeing my boy, he said the same thing: "Anybody who
   isn't happy in Paradise must be crazy." And dangerous. And
   he was right. I am dangerous. So you'd better watch out.'

DIRECTOR. Watch out. Watch out, huh? That's good advice
   for all of us. So – what do you think? Luke?

DANIEL LUCAS (*dazed*). What?

DIRECTOR. Not badly written. And life-like, huh? And
   Latinos. We could fulfil our quota. What d'you think?
   Should we give this Malko a chance?

DANIEL LUCAS *turns, as if in a trance.*

IRENE. I believe Mr. Lucas told you that he hasn't formed an
   opinion yet, sir.

DIRECTOR (*looks her over again*). Well, we have to be extra
   careful. We're being watched. We've got to authorise more,
   so our enemies can't accuse us of not being liberal enough.
   And we've got to authorise less, so they can't accuse us of
   not being conservative enough. We're at a critical moment.
   Happy but critical. Because there's only one problem with
   Paradise – one problem: people get bored. (*Pause.*) Some
   sponsors are worried because we're too lusty, risqué, racy,
   you know, and other sponsors are worried because we're too
   traditional, not enough new stuff. But they're all united in
   one common cause, right, Irene?

IRENE (*as if reciting a litany*). To never forget how the plague
   started, to heed that warning and take our punishment,
   because next time there may not be a next time.

DIRECTOR (*joining in at the end*). There may not be a next

time. Right! So we have to show where we stand. If you get my meaning?

DANIEL LUCAS. So this script. You wish me to . . . ?

DIRECTOR. Your son.

DANIEL LUCAS. What about – my – ?

DIRECTOR. Not married yet, I take it, since the last time I inquired?

DANIEL LUCAS. No, sir, you may remember he obtained a deferral due to his – He's graduating from Medicine this –

DIRECTOR. Yes – if he's studying so hard that would explain why his happy signature isn't in yet. You know, the –

IRENE. Mr. Lucas is perfectly aware of the marriage signature, sir, the one that had to be ready at noon tomorrow. He's already sent for Nicholas –

The DIRECTOR *ushers* IRENE *out of the room.*

IRENE. Alright, alright. I have to go and feed my cat anyway. Today's . . . Thursday.

She exits and remains on the other side of the anteroom door, trying to listen to the conversation.

DIRECTOR. This signature – it matters, Daniel. Because – Can you keep a secret? Can you? Well, I'm moving up, Luke. Up, up, up.

DANIEL LUCAS. How far up, sir?

DIRECTOR (*whispering*). SuperDirector. SuperPope. So –

DANIEL LUCAS. So . . . ?

DIRECTOR. So you're in the running to take over my present post. Top of the list. Unless –

DANIEL LUCAS. Unless . . . ?

DIRECTOR. Well, we can expect a lot of extra scrutiny in the days ahead, Luke. Ways in which your loyalty gets tested, you know, people going over your past with a comb to make sure that . . . But you don't have anything to worry about, do you? No abortions, right? No unhappy contraceptives being used, right?

DANIEL LUCAS. So those people, sir, they will be asking questions about . . . about my wife, sir?

DIRECTOR. What wife?

DANIEL LUCAS. My – former wife. Tanya.

DIRECTOR. What's there to ask about her?

DANIEL LUCAS. Well, that depends, sir – I mean, perhaps you've spoken – recently, I mean – to somebody about her . . .

DIRECTOR. Fuck them, Danny. Fuck them if they're spreading vile stories. Look, when I found you – there you were, trying to get an irrelevant book published, squandering your skills, freezing on the edge of the edge, farming your young Nick out to relatives – and mad, wild, Tanya, did she care? Did she know where your real talents lay? But I knew.

DIRECTOR sits DANIEL down in his chair.

DIRECTOR. And I also knew there was one slight problem to overcome if you were to give me your unerring eyes, your then young eagle eyes, one problem to overcome if you were to join us in our crusade. One problem.

DANIEL LUCAS. I don't like to talk about this.

DIRECTOR. Right! So why are we talking about this? About her? Why aren't we talking about – more important things: such as making sure, Luke, this story of ours has a happy ending.

The DIRECTOR exits. DANIEL LUCAS scratches the right side of his head with his left hand and then looks at it as if he did not recognise it. He opens the manuscript. Behind him, the MAN and TANYA appear. TANYA is still in the chair. The MAN gently invites TANYA out of her chair.

DANIEL LUCAS (*reading*). 'There is only one way out. Tell him. Tell him what happened.'

TANYA. There is only one way out. Tell him. Tell him what happened to me.

DANIEL LUCAS. No.

TANYA. Yes. Tell him about the day the Director showed up at our house. Tell him what the Director needed from you, the one thing he needed from you. Tell him how you betrayed me. Tell him it was freezing that day. Tell him.

DANIEL LUCAS. No.

TANYA. I'll make you tell him.

DANIEL LUCAS. Nothing. I'll tell him nothing, you bitch.

DANIEL, agitated, abruptly slams the text closed. TANYA *and the* MAN *disappear.*

DANIEL LUCAS. It's not true. She's the one. She's the one who betrayed me. She didn't love me enough.

A long pause. Then hesitantly, reluctantly, DANIEL LUCAS *opens the text again. As he reads, a light appears on* TANYA, *by herself in the darkness.*

DANIEL LUCAS (*reading*). 'Tell him, yes, how the woman you loved was in the way.'

TANYA. Tell him, yes, how the woman you loved was in the way.

DANIEL LUCAS turns. They kiss. She disengages. He holds onto her desperately.

TANYA. Tell him, yes, how the woman you loved was in the way. Tell him how your marriage started to break down when you accepted this job, yes, that the woman you loved couldn't stand to see you suppress the better part of yourself. And then tell him how they asked for proof of your loyalty. What you did to her to prove your loyalty.

DANIEL LUCAS. That's not how it was.

TANYA. If you once loved . . . .

DANIEL LUCAS. Yes. A long time ago – I loved someone. But there's nothing left. I can't even remember what it felt like.

TANYA. Do you remember that poem? You read it to me the first time we made love. I was so unsure of what was in the pit of your mind and you answered: 'Love consists of this/ A dialogue of solitudes.' Don't be afraid. For once in your life, don't be afraid.

Lights begin to fade on TANYA. *She starts to leave.*

DANIEL LUCAS. Why are you saying that to me again? Why did you always say that to me?

TANYA (*as the light fades on her*). I said it so you wouldn't betray me.

DANIEL LUCAS. You betrayed me. You're the one.

Normal lights come back on the office.

DANIEL LUCAS. She's the one. She's the one who betrayed me.

DANIEL *opens the text again, peeks at it.* NICK *enters the anteroom. He is played by the same actor who played* ENRIQUE, *but conservatively dressed. He enters* DANIEL's *office.* DANIEL *looks up, startled.* NICK *goes over to give his father a hug.* DANIEL *nervously puts the manuscript away.*

NICK. Well, aren't we secretive today?

DANIEL LUCAS. Yes. Some of us are.

NICK. So – what's up? I've left three dying patients to . . .

DANIEL LUCAS. David Malko. Your friend David Malko. Tell me about him.

NICK. Never heard of.

DANIEL LUCAS (*more and more agitated*). You must know him, have talked to him at some point. Think. A writer called Malko! You told him something about my – my habits, my – wife.

NICK. Your wife?

DANIEL LUCAS. My life. You described me. Think!

NICK. My Lord, who is this Malko person who's got you so – ?

DANIEL LUCAS. Somebody's been talking about me to him – somebody's been telling him that I – What have you told your friends about me?

NICK. Nothing. Your favourite word, Dad. Nothing.

DANIEL LUCAS. Nothing, nothing. You never whispered a word about me?

NICK. The most I've ever told anybody is that you're one serious guy – serious as the smile of hell, in fact.

DANIEL LUCAS. Serious as the smile of hell? Wait. You – Malko. You got that stupid phrase from him.

NICK. It's a song, Dad. Everybody sings it. What's there to fear? What's there to fear? Nothing is as serious as the smile of hell. It is sort of stupid, but . . .

DANIEL LUCAS. You're not telling me the – In here, in this novel, there's a young man who has spent his whole life making believe he – but he's involved in . . .

NICK. Involved in what?

DANIEL LUCAS . . . . involved in something, like you – you know, with your friends. No matter what it is – you can trust me, it hasn't been easy, I've tried to be a father –

NICK. Yes, Dad – and a mother, I know. But what is it that I'm supposed to have –

DANIEL LUCAS. Don't say it. Not another word. Not in here. They're watching us.

NICK. Here? In the office of Mr. Loyalty? Who's –

DANIEL. The tree police.

NICK. What tree police? Hey what's –

The intercom buzzes.

DANIEL LUCAS (*answering*). Oh, yes, Director . . . . He's here right now. I'll get it as soon as I hang up, sir. Yes. Tomorrow at noon.

DANIEL LUCAS *hangs up, turns to* NICK.

Well, here's your chance. He wants the marriage signature. Before noon tomorrow. You sign and that proves that all my suspicions are wrong.

NICK. What suspicions? Just because I'm not sure about this marriage thing – Yesterday we had agreed that we could defer –

DANIEL LUCAS. We can't wait. No more deferments. I'm – being tested. You have to sign. Or they'll –

NICK. They'll what? Listen, Dad, if that computer makes a –

DANIEL LUCAS. The computer never makes a mistake. It
unfailingly matches the right young man with the right
young woman. Right genes, right attitudes, right breeding
yields the right children. Look at you. Look at your mother
and me, look at how well that –

NICK. How can you be sure?

DANIEL LUCAS. What do you mean?

NICK. Was it really that successful, your marriage?

DANIEL LUCAS. How can you ask me that? You know that
she died holding my hand, that we – Who's been telling you
. . . ?

NICK. C'mon, Dad. Nobody's been – I just asked you
because, well, she did die young, before you had a chance
to find out if it was going to – Nobody's told me a thing.

DANIEL. I don't deserve this runaround. Somebody's out to
get me, Nick, and if they're spreading rumours . . . Nick!
Please. You've got to help me.

NICK *hands a photo to* DANIEL LUCAS, *who examines it.*

NICK. Mom's photo. I think it's her photo. It arrived this
morning, Dad. In the mail. I decided I wouldn't even bring
it to your – but if there's a campaign against you – Look at
what's written on the other side. 'Once upon a time there
was a man who was afraid.'

DANIEL LUCAS (*turns it over, reads*). Afraid? Afraid of
what? What is this? Some sort of sick joke? Who wrote
this?

NICK (*calmly*). You tell me. Is there something you're afraid
of?

DANIEL LUCAS (*agitated*). Nothing, nothing.

As NICK *answers, the* MAN *appears on the other side of
the stage. He makes a gesture. We see* TANYA.

NICK. Then there's no reason to be this upset, right? Unless –
unless . . . There is something you – something to do with
mom. Why else would somebody go to all the trouble of

finding her photo and then sending it and then – Dad? Is there something you're afraid of?

Lights begin to fade on NICK, *grow stronger on* TANYA.

DANIEL LUCAS (*barely in control*). I told you. Nothing. You heard me. I said nothing. Nothing. Nothing. Nothing. My God – I've got to get out of here.

NICK (*almost a shadow*). Is there something you haven't – Did something – did something happen to my mother?

DANIEL. I've got to get out. I – your mother, your mother. I've got to get out.

NICK *disappears.*

NICK's VOICE. Dad? What happened to my mother?

Lights go down on the office. A spot on DANIEL, *who doesn't move. He is paralysed by fear. He clutches the umbrella in his hand as if it were a weapon. The* MAN *crosses towards him.*

MAN (*casually*). I've been thinking about pain. There is good pain and there is bad pain. Good pain is at the origin of all knowledge, it's – good for you. Knowing where we begin and others end. There are good borders and then there are bad borders. Borders that preserve who we are and borders that let in the germs of who we are not. So when boundaries are violated, when rules are broken, just remember there's somebody like me who's there. At the edge. You fuck with the edge. You fuck with me.

The MAN *turns, makes a gesture,* TANYA *comes forward.*

TANYA. Tell him how you betrayed me.

Murky, swirling lights surround DANIEL LUCAS, *as he speaks and slowly becomes* DON ALFONSO MORALES.

DANIEL LUCAS (*to himself, whispering*). It's not true. She was the one. She was the one who betrayed me – by hating what I – by not even trying to co-operate. And why the hell was she there anyway? That day. That day I came home and Tanya was there. I don't know how she got in. I didn't even ask her. Crazy: she was combing her hair. (*To* TANYA, *who has started to comb her long hair.*) What are you doing here?

DON ALFONSO *limps towards her, helping himself with the umbrella. He is gentle with her, as if she needed care.*

TANYA. I'm making myself pretty to see my little boy.

DON ALFONSO. He'll be back from school any time now. It would be better if you left before –

TANYA. They know who I am. They can see under my face. Here – touch the plague under my face. Touch me here, under my face and feel the –

DON ALFONSO. You're crazy.

TANYA. Anybody who isn't happy in Paradise must be crazy, right? That's what that Judge said when he stopped me from seeing my boy. But that wasn't enough for you, was it?

DON ALFONSO. You need help. Professional help.

TANYA. Well, they came for me this morning. Your friend the Director. He was with them. He had my signature. Confessing. Accepting my guilt. Accepting that I would spend the rest of my life in a loony –

DON ALFONSO. Don't call it that.

TANYA. Only it wasn't my signature. Guess who signed for me?

DON ALFONSO. I did it to save you. They would have dragged it out of you. They would have hurt you.

TANYA. So that's what you said to yourself when you signed for me. In the name of others, in the name of Paradise – isn't that what they always say? Over and over again in history, isn't that the excuse? For the good of others?

The MAN appears out of the darkness with the chair, sets it down, steps back, watches the scene. Only we see him.

DON ALFONSO. Yes, Tanya – it was for your good. They would have come for you anyway and I –

TANYA. They don't know where I am now.

DON ALFONSO. Then you'd better leave before they find out.

TANYA. Not until I've said good-bye to my boy. Not until I've told him the truth.

DON ALFONSO. You never knew when to stop. You asked for it.

DON ALFONSO turns his back on TANYA, takes a cellular phone out of his pocket, begins to speak. She circles him, trying to catch his eye while he continues to turn his back.

DON ALFONSO. Get me the Director.

TANYA. I wouldn't call him if I were you.

DON ALFONSO. Ah, Director. Not too well, I'm afraid. In fact, I'm having a spot of trouble – the bitch is right here, in fact.

TANYA. You're not going to stop me.

DON ALFONSO. I'll keep her here, Director. Just hurry.

DON ALFONSO hangs up.

TANYA (*breaking down*). Please, Alfonso.

DON ALFONSO starts to calm her down, kisses her gently, then suddenly pins her arms and sits her down in the chair.

TANYA. No. No. I won't let you shut me up – I won't, I won't –

DON ALFONSO starts to gag her.

TANYA (*gasping for breath*). You crippled son of a bitch! I'll be back for my boy.

I'll tell him what you –

DON ALFONSO finishes gagging her.

DON ALFONSO. You'll tell him nothing, you bitch. Nothing. Nothing.

Lights begin to go down on TANYA in her chair. Suddenly, the DIRECTOR surges forward. He stands next to TANYA, looks at DON ALFONSO for a few beats, then drags her away into the darkness. DON ALFONSO watches, shocked. He staggers backward, into the space of the darkened office. As the lights change, he becomes DANIEL LUCAS again, returns to the position he occupied before, looking at the photo.

NICK'S VOICE (*from the darkness*). I asked you a question.

The lights return to normal.

DANIEL LUCAS. What question?

NICK. What happened to my mother?

DANIEL LUCAS. Nothing. Nothing. What I always told you.
She died in our house. I was holding her hand when she –

NICK. Yes, yes, I've heard it all before – how you tried to be
a father and a mother to me. Only not this time. This time
I know you're hiding something.

DANIEL. You mustn't believe the stories people are –
circulating. I have enemies. They don't want me to be
promoted, they –

NICK. Maybe they know something I should know.

DANIEL. Excuse me. I have work to do. I can be monitored at
any moment to see if my work is satisfactory.

DANIEL *picks up the manuscript, begins to sharpen a
pencil: empty gestures to avoid looking at* NICK.

NICK. Dad? Dad? Whoever sent that photo knows. He'll tell
me. He'll tell me what happened to my mother.

NICK *exits. Lights begin to go down leaving a strong beam
on* DANIEL LUCAS.

DANIEL LUCAS. Lies, Nick. All lies.

DANIEL *picks up the manuscript and reads it. Or his voice
could be pre-recorded and come out of the darkness.*

DANIEL LUCAS (*reading or in off*). 'So you thought you
knew him, Alfonso? You brought him up, but did you know
him, that motherless mystery of a young man?

A bed appears. IRENE *is in it.* DANIEL *moves towards it
slowly.*

He's farther from you than the remotest star, farther from
you than your own image reflected in the only eyes that want
to reflect your tired features, Jacqueline's loyal eyes.' And
Don Alfonso Morales remembered without enthusiasm . . .

DANIEL LUCAS *has reached the bed. He throws the
manuscript down on the bed. He begins to undress. She
begins to read.*

IRENE (*reading*). 'And Don Alfonso remembered without enthusiasm that he was scheduled to meet Jacqueline again –
another monotonous Thursday night encounter he would
honour only because our fearful friend had no other unfortunate body in this desolate universe to welcome him.
And he realised that he didn't trust her, that he could not
tell her his most secret thoughts. That he did not love her.'

IRENE *looks up at him. He gets into bed. Semi-darkness.*
Frustrated love-making, DANIEL *saying: I can't, I can't,*
IRENE *urging him on,* DANIEL *cursing,* IRENE *trying to*
calm him down.

DANIEL LUCAS. I'm sorry. God, I'm sorry.

IRENE. What's there to be sorry about?

DANIEL LUCAS. Well – the thing didn't – you know – well –
work.

DANIEL LUCAS *flicks the lamp on.*

IRENE. Does it matter that much? Men are always so worried
about –

DANIEL LUCAS. Don't try to disguise that I was not quite up
to standards.

IRENE. You were – well, strange, if you're so hot to know.
As if I were making love with – well, trying to make love –
with someone I had just met.

DANIEL LUCAS. So you also found me strange?

IRENE. Somebody else found you strange?

DANIEL LUCAS. Nicholas.

IRENE. What sort of – performance did he complain about?

DANIEL LUCAS. That's not funny. My performance with you
was not what might be – expected, simply because of that
infernal novel.

IRENE. Mr. Malko's?

DANIEL LUCAS. That's the culprit.

IRENE. It's his real name. Not a pseudonym. And I got you
the address. Here it is. Hasn't got a phone. Lives out in the

slums. No job. Had to ship his kid to his wife's parents because they couldn't afford to – They barely get by on what his wife –

DANIEL LUCAS. So our friend Malko's not doing too well.

DANIEL LUCAS *starts to dress.*

IRENE. You seem to enjoy the idea that he's in trouble.

DANIEL LUCAS. Yes, I do. I hope he's in bushels of trouble. What right does the rascal have to inject me into his libellous book? Or to steal my thoughts, my most secret thoughts?

IRENE. Well. (*Pause.*) Maybe there's a little something in Malko's novel you're keeping from me? Let's forget the monotonous Thursday encounters and the unfortunate body. Here. Don Alfonso is – thinking – ha! – to himself. (IRENE *reads from the manuscript.*) 'Got to go and see Jacqueline now. She's possessive and obtuse – but at least she's got splendid breasts. If I cared for her . . . ' Now, what's this to do with us? The breasts, I'll accept that part of it, I rather like that part, but possessive and obtuse . . . and then it says he doesn't love her . . .

DANIEL LUCAS. Care for her.

IRENE. Always correcting, always correcting. Care for her, love her. You underlined that part.

DANIEL LUCAS. I merely underlined it because it was one of the few places that did not fit me, fit our little –

IRENE. Our little . . . So where she says, You don't trust me. That has nothing to do with us? I read that too, Daniel – and it – Maybe this story's telling me that you're – You don't trust me, do you?

Thunder. Outside the room, under a murky ghostly light, two shadows begin to emerge, one seated in a chair, the other behind the chair. We cannot see who they are.

As she says: Your silence is eloquent.

DANIEL LUCAS. Silence is never eloquent, woman – Oh my God – You're the one. I know, I know: now you're going to tell me that the bitch came today to –

IRENE. What bitch came today?

DANIEL LUCAS. You're the one. You're the one who –

IRENE. I'm the one who what? What am I doing except hitching my ass to a man who won't marry me?

DANIEL LUCAS. You're the one who's been telling them. About Tanya.

IRENE. About Tanya?

DANIEL LUCAS. About me, about me.

IRENE (*derisively*). Sorry to contradict you, honey, but that theory won't hold water, not a drop of it. Why would I want to screw up our relationship more. It's already in enough trouble. If you're looking for someone you'd never suspect-

Thunder. Rain starts. DANIEL *turns to the window. Outside, one of the shadows turns into* NICK, *seated in the same chair* TANYA *occupied before, gagged and tied like she was, under a beam of white light. Behind him, the* MAN.

IRENE . . . . How about Nick?

DANIEL LUCAS *is upset, peering at the shadows.*

IRENE. I mean, what if Nick is – well, involved in something? Following orders – you know, from the free-fuck conspiracy or some other nutty organisation?

MAN (*to* NICK). So you want to know what happened to your mother, huh? Well, I never had a mother. So I guess I'm in a position to tell you what happened to yours. Wouldn't you say? If you could say? Or maybe, if you could say something, you'd like to tell me something else. Before you find out what happened to your mother.

DANIEL LUCAS. No. No. Leave him alone. Don't –

MAN (*to* NICK). Just remember: I'm your friend. Your only friend.

IRENE. What's the matter, Daniel?

DANIEL LUCAS (*moving towards the door*). I'll save him. I won't let . . .

Lights dim slightly on IRENE *as she starts dressing and* DANIEL LUCAS *rushes out.* NICK *and the* MAN *suddenly*

disappear, leaving the rain and the silence. A long pause.
The rain stops. Suddenly, the DIRECTOR *appears.*
DANIEL LUCAS *crosses to him.*

DANIEL LUCAS. Director, Director!

DIRECTOR. I'm not the damn director of anything.

DANIEL LUCAS. In that case, you must – excuse me, sir.
I must be – I haven't been – well lately –

DIRECTOR. These things happen. Mistaken identities, I mean.
I've been confused before with somebody else.

DANIEL LUCAS. Alright, sir, I get it – it's a test, I understand.

DIRECTOR. I hate tests. Ever since school. When I had to get
my father's signature on every lousy test. He beat the shit
out of me. All because of a signature.

DANIEL LUCAS. The signature. Of course. Noon. Tomorrow.
My Nick's a good boy, sir, a bit stubborn, you know, young
people –

DIRECTOR. I don't know any young people. But it sounds to
me as if this little Nick of yours is in trouble. As if he's up
to no good.

DANIEL LUCAS. I'm afraid I don't understand.

DIRECTOR. You're afraid. Good for you. Fear is the root of
all wisdom.

The DIRECTOR *exits.* DANIEL LUCAS *makes an attempt*
to follow – then stops. IRENE, *having dressed, joins him in*
the street.

DANIEL LUCAS (*to* IRENE, *wildly*). The Director – the
Director – He was just here, he – He's after my boy, he's –

IRENE. You must be dreaming. The Director has a chauffeur.
And why would he be on the streets looking for Nick?

DANIEL LUCAS. He said he wasn't the Director, but –

IRENE. You see.

DANIEL LUCAS. It's that damn book. It's driving me crazy.
I'm – seeing things.

IRENE. Trap the bastard!

DANIEL LUCAS. The Director?

IRENE. Malko. David Malko. Listen, honey, if somebody were fucking with my identity, I'd tear their eyes out. Let's track him down, this Malko bastard, find out who he's working for, who's feeding him his information. Your co-facilitators, or Nick, or – who knows –

DANIEL LUCAS. Track him down?

The sound of a typewriter. Lights rise on the MALKO *house, showing it to be sombre and poor. The silhouette of a woman appears, typing. We cannot distinguish her face yet.*

DANIEL LUCAS. Irene, I'm going to do it. They want to drive me mad? Well, I'll do something mad, something they'll – I'll find out if Nick is part of this – this – (*Speaking as he walks towards the* MALKO *house.*) Cover for me at the office. I'll be back as soon as I find out who's been spying on me, writing me down, who it is, and why. As soon as I –

IRENE. As soon as you – what, my love?

DANIEL LUCAS *has reached the* MALKO *door.*

DANIEL LUCAS. As soon I find out how this damn story ends.

DANIEL LUCAS *knocks on the door. The lights go up on* SONIA, *typing. She is played by the same actress who plays* TANYA, *except her hair is tucked away with a scarf. She wears heavy winter clothes, as if it were very cold and there were no heating in the room. Another knock. Total darkness.*

End of Act One.

ACT TWO

In the darkness, the sound of typing. Then, knocking. Lights rise on DANIEL LUCAS *in front of* MALKO's *house. Another knock. The sound of typing stops. Another knock. We can vaguely see the figure of a man, also wrapped in heavy clothes, next to* SONIA. *He is* DAVID MALKO, *but we cannot yet distinguish his face.*

DAVID (*whispering, shivering*). Don't open.

SONIA (*whispering*). I have to. They heard me typing.

DAVID (*rubbing himself with his arms, as if cold*). Let's keep on writing. Sonia. Damn. If I had permission for a computer . . .

SONIA. Quiet!

SONIA crosses to the door, as DAVID *sits at the typewriter. She opens halfway. She can see* DANIEL LUCAS, *but he cannot see her yet.*

DANIEL LUCAS (*shy*). David Malko?

SONIA (*suspicious*). He's not in. (*Pause.*)

DANIEL LUCAS. I'm – a publisher. A friend of Bergante's. He – suggested this visit. (*Pause.*) I've read the novel.

SONIA hesitates, then opens. DANIEL LUCAS *is astonished to see someone who so resembles* TANYA.

SONIA. Please come in. I'm Mrs. Malko – but you can call me Sonia.

DANIEL LUCAS *doesn't move.*

SONIA. Is there something wrong?

DANIEL LUCAS *leans against the door, as if he were about to faint.*

DANIEL LUCAS (*weakly*). Nothing. It's – a dizzy spell, I get them some – For a moment, I thought – I thought –

(*Recovering.*) A mere coincidence. Meaningless as dreams.

SONIA (*turns, entering the room*). Love, this gentleman . . .
Mr . . . . Mr . . . .

DANIEL LUCAS *comes into the austere, cold room. Lights
rise and we see that* DAVID MALKO *is played by the same
actor who plays* NICK *and* ENRIQUE, *but he has glasses
on.* DAVID *sits at the typewriter. He unwraps his arms,
begins to type furiously.* DANIEL LUCAS *is stunned at this
second resemblance, falls into a chair.*

SONIA. He's a publisher. A friend of Bergante's – But he's –
I'm afraid you really are not well, sir. (*Pause.*). Maybe a
cup of coffee would do you –

DANIEL LUCAS. It's nothing, I'll be – I'll be . . . This is the
house of – You are – David Malko?

DAVID *gets up from the machine, shakes* DANIEL's *hand.*

DAVID. Who else would I be? Unemployed, working with my
merciless characters – Malko Incorporated. Hey – you look
as if you'd seen a ghost.

SONIA. David!

DAVID. Well, he does.

SONIA. Our – guest has read 'Turns,' David.

DAVID. Well, he's going to be the only one –

SONIA. There you go again – always so negative. If you want
to be successful, write something different, but don't
complain all day long –

DAVID (*to* DANIEL LUCAS). Didn't Bergante say it was
hopeless? Isn't that what that guy called the Pope said?

DANIEL LUCAS (*beginning to recover*). The – Pope?

DAVID. 'Cause he's infallible, they say.

DANIEL LUCAS. And Bergante gave you no other details
about this – ?

DAVID. Only that everybody calls him the Pope. And that it
was hopeless.

SONIA *sits down behind* DAVID, *looks fixedly at* DANIEL LUCAS.

DANIEL LUCAS. You give up hope too easily, Mr. – Malko. Your characters would never accept defeat so –

DAVID. Yeah, but they're fiction.

DANIEL LUCAS. But quite – well life-like, wouldn't you say? I mean, your characters – this – Don Alfonso, ah, Morales I think it is, he must be modelled on someone real, someone must have told you about –

DAVID. Well, I'm glad someone thinks the son of a bitch is life-like. I think he's pretty lifeless, if you want my opinion, but he's not modelled on –

DANIEL LUCAS. That woman then, she –

DAVID. What woman?

DANIEL LUCAS. The mother, Tanya, the one who returns, that one –

DAVID. This guy doesn't read very closely, does he? The mother's not called – Tanya. She hasn't got a name. Dead people don't have names.

DANIEL LUCAS. So she's dead? She is dead, that woman, isn't – ?

DAVID. Hey, did you read – See, Sonia, they don't understand a fuck – that's what happens when the only ones who get to read you are censors –

DANIEL LUCAS. What censors?

DAVID. Bastards! Fifty years controlling every adjective in the universe with the pretext of saving us from plagues they made themselves.

DANIEL LUCAS. You young people – you don't understand, do you, what things were like before our parents instituted these restrictions on – democratically instituted –

DAVID. Democratically – so most of the people are idiots, most of the people want to get screwed, does that – ?

DANIEL LUCAS. Idiots? The idiots were the ones who would not accept sacrifices to stop the plague, to secure the streets, secure our bodies. I've studied what it was like: the moaning naked women plastered on every screen, the children saturated with sex and violence and vulgarity, the poor incited to aggression and despair by wild savage music, the lack of tradition and discipline corroding the very fabric of –

DAVID (*stands up, agitated*). Bullshit! Bullshit publicity. I'm surprised a friend of Bergante's would swallow such – Hey, why did old Bergante send you anyway?

SONIA. You must forgive my husband, sir. He's –

DAVID. Answer the question or get the fuck out!

DANIEL LUCAS. Bergante wants to know – when your novel will be finished. And he asked about the ending, also about the ending.

DAVID. He wants a happy ending, huh?

DANIEL LUCAS. We all want a happy ending.

DAVID. Well too bad. Tell Bergante I'm not going to change a word to accommodate anyone. And if it takes a hundred years before my work gets green-lighted, then it'll –

DANIEL LUCAS (*barely controlling himself*). Mr. Malko – let me say that you would do well to learn some humbleness from your lifeless characters. Let me say no more. Though yes, yes. Accommodation to the messy world around you: An authorisation for a computer, for a preproduction budget, for a reading with actors, a contract, none of this would hurt you, would it?

DANIEL LUCAS *stands in front of* DAVID, *who is seated, both of them exactly in the same position as the* DIRECTOR *and* DANIEL LUCAS *in a previous scene.*

DAVID. Hey, are you offering me a job?

DANIEL LUCAS. No, of course not, I'm just –

DAVID. Trying to bribe me? Trying to get me to stop writing?

DANIEL LUCAS. Not at all. But if you were to change your text slightly, diminish your disparagement of what ordinary people believe – a few dialogues snipped delicately here, the softening of an idea there and –

DAVID. Not one snip, not one snap. That's how you start, and
    soon you start rewriting whole chunks –

DANIEL LUCAS. I don't see what difference a few words
    could –

DAVID. A few words? You know what, Sonia? This guy's a
    fucking ecofascist. The hell to him and to Bergante and
    while I'm at it, the hell to that Pope guy too. Fuck the lot of
    you! C'mon, honey, let's get some work done.

SONIA. David! Control yourself.

DAVID. C'mon, Sonia – it's the mother/son scene. When they
    finally meet in prison.

DANIEL LUCAS (*to himself, alarmed*). They can't meet.
    She's dead. The mother can't –

    SONIA *looks at* DANIEL, *as if she has somehow
    recognised him.*

DAVID. Maybe this guy will get bored and he'll leave. Maybe
    he'll learn a thing or two.

    DAVID *starts typing and* SONIA *collaborates with him. At
    the same time, she is looking at* DANIEL LUCAS, *as if
    speaking to him.*

SONIA. So she says: Do you know who I am?

DAVID. And so far we have Enrique saying: I've seen you
    before. Hmmm. That doesn't sound quite right. I mean –
    he's tied to a chair, right? And he's – hardly able to breathe,
    so . . .

DANIEL LUCAS (*muttering, to himself*). Oh, my God!

SONIA. But they can speak. People always manage to speak to
    each other, if they really want to.

DAVID (*typing*). Right. So what if he were to say to her: My
    dad burnt all your photographs.

SONIA. But I saw you . . .

DAVID. But I saw you in my dreams.

    DANIEL *watches* DAVID *and* SONIA *become* NICK *and*
    TANYA.

SONIA. And in those dreams did I tell you what happened to me?

DAVID. All I know is that you – came to our house that day.

SONIA. I was inside when your father arrived. I was combing my hair.

DANIEL LUCAS (*anguished*). Enough, enough! I have to go, I have to go.

DANIEL LUCAS stands, hastily, goes to the door. SONIA follows him outside. Lights go down on DAVID inside.

SONIA. I'm sorry. We've been rude.

DANIEL LUCAS. So there's – no way of saving the boy?

SONIA. It depends on what you call saving – but there are ways.

DANIEL LUCAS. How?

SONIA. Read the novel when it comes out. Or see the movie.

DANIEL LUCAS. And if I have to wait, as your husband suggested, a hundred years?

SONIA. That depends on you.

DANIEL LUCAS. I must be – It's getting late. Stormy.

SONIA. I wish you the best of luck, sir. You and your family. I hope things go well for you.

DANIEL LUCAS. I thank you for your consideration, madame, but there is no reason to believe that –

SONIA. I'm only saying it because today – I noticed that today you came without your umbrella.

DANIEL LUCAS. I do not use an umbrella, madame.

SONIA. Perhaps I confused you, sir, with someone else.

DANIEL LUCAS. Perhaps. These things do happen – confusions of this sort, I mean.

SONIA. You can trust me.

She waits. He hesitates.

DANIEL LUCAS. Many years ago . . . I – I – made – I think I made a mistake, many years ago.

SONIA. Some mistakes are not – irreparable.

DANIEL LUCAS. And some are.

SONIA. There is a saying in the town where I was born. To drive out a nail –

DANIEL LUCAS. You need another nail. Yes. A long time ago someone – she was just like you – used to say things like that.

SONIA. Did she ever tell you not to be afraid?

DANIEL LUCAS. Too many times.

SONIA. We can never say that too many times.

DANIEL LUCAS. She said it too many times. I grew to – fear her.

SONIA. I am sorry to hear that. (*Pause.*) Take care of yourself. And your son. I wish you both the best of luck. Sir.

SONIA *exits. Down the street,* DANIEL LUCAS *sees the* MAN, *waiting and watching.*

MAN. Looking for somebody?

DANIEL LUCAS. No, I –

MAN. Because I am. I am looking for somebody. If you know what I mean. I'm looking for anybody who wants to fuck with the borders. So don't. That's where meaning starts: knowing what the limit is. That's the one thing a father can teach his son. So why don't you – go home. To your son. If you have a home, that is. And if you still have a son.

DANIEL LUCAS. I'm warning you. Leave my boy alone.

MAN. I was never a boy. Were you ever a boy?

DANIEL LUCAS. What do you mean?

MAN. I don't remember ever having been a boy. In my profession, you don't need a childhood. Of course, there are some boys who never grow up. They just stay that way – forever. If you know what I mean?

DANIEL LUCAS. Who are you?

MAN. Maybe I'm your friend. Maybe I'm the only friend you've ever had. Think about it.

The MAN *exits.* DANIEL LUCAS *is desperate.*

DANIEL LUCAS. My boy. My son.

He takes out his cellular phone. He dials a number.

DANIEL LUCAS. Maybe there's still time.

Lights rise on the anteroom where IRENE *answers the phone.*

IRENE. Mr. Lucas – where have you been? The Director's been calling all morning about –

DANIEL LUCAS. Never mind him. Enrique, did he – ?

IRENE. Who?

DANIEL LUCAS. My son Nick, Nick, did he call to –

IRENE. The one who's been calling like crazy is the Director. He's asking about the signature.

DANIEL LUCAS. I'll get it for him. Just find Nick.

IRENE. Nick's here, in your office.

DANIEL LUCAS. Keep him there. Do you understand?

The lights rise on DANIEL LUCAS*'s office,* NICK *waiting inside.* DANIEL LUCAS *crosses the stage and enters the anteroom.*

IRENE. Oh, God, I'm glad you –

DANIEL LUCAS. Where's Nick? Have they come for him? Have they?

IRENE. He's in there. Get a hold of yourself.

DANIEL LUCAS. Myself?

IRENE. Where have you been?

DANIEL LUCAS. At Malko's.

IRENE. So you saw him? What did he – ?

DANIEL LUCAS. I don't know if I saw him.

IRENE. Malko? How can't you not know ?

DANIEL LUCAS. It was as if I was – I was – visiting, listen, Jacqueline –

IRENE. Jacqueline?

DANIEL . . . . as if I was visiting my own self, the man I – Quick. The book. Give it to me. I'll find out what the limping bastard is going to do –

IRENE. What limping bastard?

DANIEL LUCAS. Alfonso Morales.

IRENE. Problem is: I sent it back to Bergante this morning.

DANIEL LUCAS. But I haven't reached the part where – I need to read what they're planning – if they hunt down his son, if Nick is – that's how I'll know what –

IRENE. I told Bergante that story was – cursed, that it was affecting your – well, I didn't say your – performance, I just told him I was getting it the hell out of here.

DANIEL LUCAS. They're after him, Irene.

DANIEL LUCAS *goes into his office.*

DANIEL LUCAS. Thank God, Nick, I thought they might have already –

NICK (*cold, angry*). I know everything.

DANIEL LUCAS. What do you know?

NICK. About mom.

DANIEL LUCAS. There's nothing to – listen, Nick, what matters now is to save you, to make sure that –

NICK. I have proof.

DANIEL LUCAS. We don't have time for – If we don't keep the Director on our side, they'll – Nick, they'll –

Sound of a typewriter. Dimly lit view of DAVID MALKO's house, shadows of DAVID and SONIA. Lights on DANIEL and NICK begin to change, grow murky and swirling, enveloping DANIEL LUCAS and NICK.

NICK. They'll what – ?

DANIEL LUCAS (*as the typewriter continues*). They'll –
they'll –

NICK (*reminding us more and more of* ENRIQUE). They'll
what – what they did to my mother?

Lights go up on SONIA *in the house, seated at the
typewriter.* DAVID's *silhouette is behind her, barely
discernible.*

DANIEL LUCAS. Nobody did anything to your mother. Who
has been spreading stories about – ?

NICK. I wish they were stories. But Mom died in a
Readjustment Centre.

DANIEL LUCAS. That's a lie. Your mother died in our house.
I was with her when she –

NICK. I know what happened, Dad. Somebody – told me.

DANIEL LUCAS. Nothing happened.

NICK. Why did you send her there, Dad? What were you so
afraid of?

DANIEL LUCAS (*hesitantly*). Nothing.

The sound of the typewriter stops, the lights on the MALKO
house fade. A ghostly beam on SONIA *as she lets her hair
loose and becomes* TANYA. *She comes to them. Only*
DANIEL *can see her.*

TANYA. There's only one way out. 'Love consists of this/ A
dialogue of solitudes.'

NICK. You betrayed her, didn't you?

DANIEL LUCAS. No.

NICK. Yes, you signed her name, you gagged her, you sent for
the Director . . .

DANIEL LUCAS (*overlapping, speaking as much to* TANYA
as to NICK). No, no, no.

NICK. Yes, you watched them take her away. Didn't you?
Didn't you?

DANIEL LUCAS. Yes. Yes. Yes. (*To* TANYA.) Damn you.

TANYA *disappears.* DANIEL *collapses.*

NICK. Damn you. What happened to her? Did you kill her?

DANIEL LUCAS. After that day, I never saw her again. I
never knew what they did to her. I never tried to find out.
Years later I heard she died. That afternoon you came back
and then we went out for an ice-cream. You liked vanilla . . .
Say something . . . Don't look at me like that. I wasn't the
only one. Everybody was – Back then – you don't
understand – back then everybody did it. It was that or
accomplish nothing, watch your life go by in smoke, waste
away your life eternally on the outside, and she just
wouldn't play along, she was just – she was so – beautiful,
she was so . . . stubborn. Don't you understand? I was
afraid. We were all afraid. I believed in a cause.

The DIRECTOR *enters the anteroom, shushes* IRENE,
begins to listen outside the door.

DANIEL LUCAS. Please say something. Anything. Nick?
(*Silence.*) I wanted to save you pain.

NICK. If you wanted to save me pain, you should have killed
me when I came home that day.

The DIRECTOR *and* IRENE *enter the office. The lights
change and become normal again.*

DIRECTOR. Good morrow and good morning or would it be
more appropriate to wish you a good afternoon, Mr. Danny
Luke.

IRENE. It's 11.56, Director. Not afternoon yet.

DIRECTOR. Well, well, Irene. Learning from the master to be
mathematical. And here's our young friend Nicholas, ready
for action – Ready to find some lucky girl, some lucky
computer, ready to be one of the multitude of happy couples
honouring Our Fifty Years of Moral Resources. (*Pause.*)
So . . . ?

DANIEL LUCAS. I'll be back right away, sir.

DANIEL LUCAS *exits to the anteroom with* IRENE, *leaving* NICK *with the* DIRECTOR. *DANIEL LUCAS signs a piece of paper, while* IRENE *objects – then they both go back into the office. He hands the paper to the* DIRECTOR.

DANIEL LUCAS. High-noon, sir. The Lucas family quota.

DIRECTOR. Good for the Lucas family. I knew I could count on you. And on this boy. My congratulations, young man. Just one thing, I'm just asking for one thing. I want the first one. The first kid is mine to name and baptise and celebrate. The first – is mine.

The DIRECTOR *exults, takes out some cigars, passes them around. The chimes of the Smiley Minute begin to sound. Everybody but* NICK *automatically smiles.* DANIEL LUCAS *gives* IRENE *a hug, the* DIRECTOR *turns to* NICK *to embrace him.* NICK *takes a step backward.*

NICK. That's not my signature.

Nobody moves. Only the sound of the chimes continue for several beats, and then die out.

DANIEL LUCAS. That's Nick for you. Can't help making last minute jokes –

NICK. He forged my signature.

DIRECTOR. But why should a loyal young man like you need anybody to forge anything on his behalf, not when marriage is such a sacred sacrament –

NICK. Don't speak to me about the sacredness of marriage, you hypocrite. I know what you did to my mother. Is she alive? Or did you have her killed?

DIRECTOR. Coming from a loyal young man, these accusations –

NICK. I'm not a loyal young man.

DANIEL LUCAS. Nick!

NICK. Don't even try and protect me, you old son of a bitch.

IRENE. Nick, how dare you speak to your –

NICK. Stay out of this.

IRENE. I'm in it because –

NICK. Because the old bastard is fucking you.

IRENE. No. He's not . . .

NICK. Then he's a fool as well as a liar.

IRENE. You don't get it, do you? Your father's going to lose his job because of –

DIRECTOR. Oh, no, no, Irene, that's where you're wrong. We're giving our friend Luke here my post.

NICK. For forging my signature, you're –

DIRECTOR. Here is a man so loyal to Moral Resources that he's ready to use fraud to get his rebellious son, his only son, to commit to our Company's happy marriage policy, help replenish our depleted species. It was a test, Luke – and you passed with flying colours. And we were also testing, well, your family – right? Because we've been suspecting this little Nicholas for a long time – and now it's out in the open: you've been a member of the free love conspiracy all these years. We just needed someone to help us flush the damn traitor from our midst – and that has been your stellar role, Daniel Lucas – and the reward is – a promotion.

DANIEL LUCAS. I – I'm grateful, sir, of course – and would be even more if you could see fit to show some mercy towards my – After all, it's only one case, only this one –

DIRECTOR. I'm surprised, Daniel. As the new Director, surely you know the value of – symbols, representations, metaphors, examples.

DANIEL LUCAS. But he's – sorry, sir, he's – Aren't you, Nick?

NICK *does not say a word.*

DIRECTOR (*picking up the phone*). Yes, we've got him. Confession and all. It worked beautifully. I'll be down with him right away. (*He hangs up.*) Or would you rather they come up and drag you down the stairs?

DANIEL LUCAS. Nick. Please . . .

DIRECTOR. I think you should come and visit him later –
when he's in a more co-operative mood. Twenty-four hours,
let's say forty-eight, Daniel.

DANIEL LUCAS. Please – don't hurt the boy, don't –

DIRECTOR. Not all pain is bad, Daniel. Some pain is – well,
good for you. Hmmm. Where did I hear that? Or is it
something I read? But then – you would be the first to
agree, as new Director, sir, that you shouldn't believe
everything you read.

The DIRECTOR *begins to exit with* NICK *in custody.*

DANIEL LUCAS. Isn't there – ? Isn't there anything – I can
do?

DIRECTOR. Tell me something. If you had to choose between
possessing a man's body and possessing his soul, what
would you choose?

DANIEL LUCAS. What do you mean?

DIRECTOR (*smiling*). Every dynasty begins with a murder.
Maybe it's time you killed – Alfonso Morales.

DIRECTOR *and* NICK *exit.* DANIEL *and* IRENE *look at
each other.*

IRENE. What does he mean?

DANIEL LUCAS. He read that book. How could he have – ?
But he trapped us by using that twisted, perverted piece of
trash. Everything in it has come true so far – everything –

IRENE. Everything? So what he said about your – wife . . . ?

DANIEL LUCAS. Irene – I – we shouldn't talk about this –
now is not the –

IRENE. 'All these years, he did not trust Jacqueline with his
secrets.' Is that also true? That you don't love me?

DANIEL LUCAS. No, of course, I –

IRENE (*with great tenderness*). 'Love consists in this/ That
two solitudes protect/'

DANIEL LUCAS (*embracing her*). 'And touch and greet each other.'

IRENE. You said that to your wife. And then you betrayed her. How can I be sure you won't betray me?

DANIEL LUCAS. Damn lies. Damn lies in that damn book. Bring me form 492.

IRENE. Form 492?

DANIEL LUCAS. Yes. Denies the author access to any possible publication, production, contract – till the day he dies. Forever. Jails him if he writes one more word.

IRENE. That's your answer? To ban the book and forbid the author because he's writing the truth about you? That's your way of proving you love me?

DANIEL LUCAS. That's the way I'll prove that Malko's damn book hasn't got any power over me. Make sure it'll never come true. I'm being tested, Irene, tested. My son's in danger, and somebody who knows everything about me wants to poison our relationship – I've got to kill Alfonso Morales.

The sound of a typewriter, Lights rise on DAVID MALKO *typing.* SONIA *looks over his shoulder. Murky, swirling lights on* DANIEL *and* IRENE *as they gradually become* DON ALFONSO *and* JACQUELINE.

IRENE. And what if you were to – what if you were to release the book? What if that is the real test? Release it, prove you've changed, you won't ever betray me? You have the power to do it – you're the Director now. They can't know it's released until it's too late. Alfonso? Are you listening to me?

DON ALFONSO *limps towards her, agitated, moves in the direction of the typewriter, comes back, stops, scratches his head.*

DON ALFONSO. I can release it without their knowing, yes, but then what? Once it's out there, do you know what they'll do to me, to Enrique? Do you know what they'll do to you?

DAVID (*in front of the typewriter*). Okay. We've got Don Alfonso Morales scratching his head. He's ready to kill. He looks at her, he says (*typing*): This damn story is eating my mind up.

DON ALFONSO (*scratching his head*). It's eating my mind up. I've got to get rid of it.

SONIA. So what if Jacqueline says: Alfonso. But you can't.

JACQUELINE. But you can't.

DAVID (*typing*). But you can't. You can't betray your dignity. No, too sentimental. Too obvious. You can't betray your –

DON ALFONSO. I can't betray my –

SONIA. Son?

DAVID. That'll come later. Maybe just keep it like that, not give it away so soon. You can't betray your – betray your –

JACQUELINE. You can't betray your – betray your –

DON ALFONSO. The person I once wanted to be? Is that what you're saying, that I can't betray the person I once wanted to be?

DAVID. I've got it. The person I once – once wanted to be. That's what Don Alfonso answers.

SONIA. Then Jacqueline says: Whatever your decision, just remember you have to live with it from now on.

DAVID (*typing*). . . . remember you have to live with it from now on.

DON ALFONSO. Yes. Live with it from now on.

JACQUELINE. Forever. Just like you have to live with what you did to her.

DON ALFONSO. But if I release it, if I . . . if I . . . .

ALFONSO *and* JACQUELINE *freeze. A long moment of silence.*

DIRECTOR's VOICE (*from the darkness*). What did he say? (*Silence.*)

The lights rise on the DIRECTOR.

DIRECTOR. Did I hear him say: But if I release it, if I . . .
If I . . . What does that mean? (*Silence.*) David? (*Silence.*)
I'm talking to you, David Malko.

DAVID *turns to him, says nothing.*

DIRECTOR. Do you know who I am?

DAVID (*slowly*). I always thought you might come. Someone
like you.

DIRECTOR. So. Why am I here, David?

DAVID. You've come – to impose order.

The DIRECTOR *walks over to* DAVID.

DIRECTOR. To impose order, sir.

DAVID. To impose order, sir.

DIRECTOR. Right. Because somebody in your fucking story
does something, then somebody in fucking reality does the
exact same thing, over and over, – and vice-versa, like
germs crisscrossing borders as if they were water – so how
do you explain that? Or do you expect me to just sit back
and just watch that happen, tell me that, wait for Danny
Lucas to betray me the way you've got Alfonso Morales
betraying his boss?

DAVID. It's – it was just fiction, sir. A – metaphor.

DIRECTOR. But I didn't write it. Did I write? So you tell me.
What happens next? (*The* DIRECTOR *reads from the
typewriter.*) Alfonso asks: Have you thought of the consequences? Good question. And our Jacqueline answers . . .
Let's see. What does Jacqueline answer. Sonia?

SONIA. We'll deal with the consequences later.

DIRECTOR. And that's as far as it goes. Not another word.
Blank page. Waiting to be written. Like an undiscovered
country. So – what do we do now?

DAVID. Were you asking – me, sir?

DIRECTOR. Who else could I be asking? What happens next?

The DIRECTOR *comes up behind* DAVID, *strips him of his
upper layers of clothing, leaving him naked from the waist*

up. DAVID *shivers, rubs himself with his arms.* DON
ALFONSO *watches.*

DIRECTOR. I'll tell you what we're going to do. We're going
to write something – together. A little, little collaboration.
Have our Don Alfonso ban the book.

DAVID. Sir?

DIRECTOR. Have him ban it. Write it down. Don Alfonso
bans the damn book.

SONIA. I don't think we can – write that.

DIRECTOR. Oh, you'll write it.

The DIRECTOR *sits* SONIA *in a chair.*

DIRECTOR. In your story, David, you allow Enrique to
heroically suffer during his interrogation, but you didn't put
him to the ultimate test. Because what's really intolerable,
David, is pain done to others. Your mother, your sweetheart,
your wife. Anything female will finally do. Anything that
can give birth will do.

SONIA. Don't do it.

DAVID. Sonia!

SONIA. Don't let them do this to us, David.

The DIRECTOR *gags* SONIA.

DIRECTOR. Everything human eventually co-operates.
(*Silence.*) Remember Tanya?

The DIRECTOR *takes* DAVID*'s hand and puts it on*
SONIA*'s breast.*

DIRECTOR. What's that called? (*Pause.*) Definitely not a
bosom. (*Pause.*) This man bans the bastard. You write it or
she writes it. Just a few words. Come on. What do a few
words matter, huh?

DAVID *types on the typewriter.*

DAVID (*haltingly*). Our hero bans the story.

DIRECTOR. Right! Back we go!

The MAN *appears in a beam of light, crosses to* DON ALFONSO *and places him in the position and the moment when* DANIEL LUCAS *said 'Damn lies. Damn lies in that damn book.' The* MAN *moves* JACQUELINE *to occupy the position* IRENE *did in that scene.*

DIRECTOR. Bring me form 492!

DON ALFONSO. Bring me form 492.

JACQUELINE. Form 492?

DON ALFONSO. Yes. Denies the author access to any possible publication, production, contract – till the day he dies.

DIRECTOR. Forever.

DON ALFONSO. Forever. Jails him if he writes one more word.

The DIRECTOR *hands* JACQUELINE *the form, she hands the form to* DON ALFONSO, *who sits behind his desk.*

DIRECTOR. Right. So now everything's back to normal.

MAN (*gesturing to* DAVID *and* SONIA). How about these two?

DIRECTOR. Well, it doesn't really matter anymore. I mean, they've got nothing more to say, have they? Not one snip, not one snap, huh, David? Where's your arrogance now, David Malko, famous author?

The DIRECTOR *makes a gesture. Blackout on* DAVID MALKO's *house. Then the lights come on again.* DAVID *and* SONIA *have disappeared.*

DIRECTOR. You want to know what happened? Maybe we offered our unknown author a job, maybe he's snipping and snapping in some office right now, maybe he'll be Director a couple of decades from now – or maybe, well, something else happened, and we don't need to know what – the guidelines say no violence, they say no blood. Quiet and discreet. As long as we don't hear from them again. Now for the good news. The boy is saved. Don Alfonso Morales has saved his son! Or would we rather . . . . ?

DIRECTOR *gestures like a magician. Elsewhere on the stage, a piercing light falls on* ENRIQUE, *who twists and screams silently.*

DIRECTOR. Now I'd say this is definitely better.

The DIRECTOR *makes another gesture, the lights black out and* ENRIQUE *is bathed in a soft colourful light, in perfect health.*

ENRIQUE (*cheerful*). Thanks, Dad. They're letting me go. They're fixing everything. Forgetting, erasing everything I said –

DIRECTOR. Rewrites! Rewrites! Forgetting, erasing everything he said, anything you said. Back we go. We get rid of all that melodramatic junk. I mean, who wants to hear him say:

ENRIQUE. If you wanted to save me pain, you should have killed me when I came home that day.

DIRECTOR. Melodramatic. Doesn't make the cut. Those lines end up on the cutting-room floor. Gone. In fact, we're getting rid of that whole scene – definitely not a family value. So when you, my friend, told your son: 'I held her hand while she died.' What Enrique answers is :

ENRIQUE. That must have been hard, Dad. But – we made it. You've been like a mother to me.

DIRECTOR. That's it. We don't want uncomfortable readers or audiences or sponsors. They need things tied neatly together. So – one finishing touch, an inspiring finale that – let's see – with this lovely piece of a woman, this pretty baby, we've left you out in the cold all this while, Jacqueline love. Let's have some romantic music, something that'll move the audience to tears – come on, come on –

Romantic strings waft through the air.

DIRECTOR. A surprise ending. Our boy here and our girl here are going to marry. The computer's found that they are just right for each other. Keep each other out of trouble.

The DIRECTOR *frantically stages the scene, dragging*
ENRIQUE *to* JACQUELINE*'s side, setting up a take,*
getting rid of office furniture.

Our hero never really loved her anyway, but to make sure
we don't lose any ratings – our Alfonso gives her up,
blesses the happy young couple. C'mon, c'mon. We're
rolling here. I want a light on this man.

A dim light comes on ALFONSO.

When I say a light, I mean a real light. For a real man,
father, player. Not a wimpy, wavering light. A killer of a
light.

The DIRECTOR *raises his arms like a magician and strong*
lights illuminate ALFONSO.

There! Bless you, my children. C'mon. Let's hear it. Bless
you my children. Alfonso!

DON ALFONSO (*with difficulty*). Bless you, my – children.

DIRECTOR. Hey, you two, let's show some passion. Only two
seconds though. And no body contact, erections, now, we
want to keep this chaste, keep it subtle. What if you place
your hand discreetly on her womb, huh? Hope the public
realises that your first grandchild is on its way. And if they
begin to feel that you are stranded, left alone – why, another
surprise turn – We'll bring Tanya back – or whatever she's
called – from the insane asylum or from the dead or
wherever she is – bring her back repentant, part of our
collective happy wedding ceremony in our new Moral
Resources stadium.

DON ALFONSO. Please, sir . . . .

DIRECTOR. Cut. Cut. Is that line in the script? Did I write
that motherfucker? You – quiet – I want no noise while this
scene is being – I'm surprised you're not – well, happy, Alf,
my boy.

DON ALFONSO. Happy?

DIRECTOR. Alright, right, so you're a bit upset – you feel that
I've been setting you up, that I fed your son information,

sent him your wife's photo, you feel I've been playing with you all this time. But it's been for your own good, the only way to test you, show you who was really trying to manipulate you, your son, that hack-writer and his wife, trying to confuse you, melt the borders of your identity, drive you insane so you would release their subversive, contagious story into the world. I've been set up as the villain of this tale – and I can tell you I'm fucking tired of it. All I'm doing is taking care of you, just as I promised the day I came to offer you this job. And Alfonso: you're the one who taught me how to fix each story so they all come out nicely, I'm only following your example, Old Eagle Eyes, snipping and snapping at other people's work just like you've been doing all your life. And I didn't hear anyone objecting then. (*To the audience.*) As a matter of fact, I don't hear any objection now either. Do I? Good. Now, where were we? Ah yes. What seems to be missing is our heroine. Some words of endearment? (JACQUELINE *says nothing.*) Well, our lady love here is embarrassed and I can't say I blame her. But blushing acceptance simply isn't enough. We need your voice, darling: Alfonso, thank you for being such a man about this. Jacqueline? Alfonso, thank you for being –

JACQUELINE. Alfonso, it doesn't have to be like this.

DIRECTOR. Wrong lines, honey.

JACQUELINE. Alfonso, don't let them do this to us.

DIRECTOR. Don't flub your lines, woman.

JACQUELINE (*angry*). I'm not flubbing anything. These are *my* lines.

DIRECTOR. Look who's suddenly full of literary pretensions.

JACQUELINE. Yes, look who's suddenly speaking. Nobody expects it of me and it's not in anybody's novel or script but I also have a story to tell. Once in a while the little little people do have stories to tell. Even the people who get their asses pinched in the hallways, even we have something to say, especially if it's about where we end up.

DIRECTOR. So you want a different ending? Why didn't you say so? I could accommodate you quite pleasurably.

DIRECTOR *fondles* JACQUELINE. *She kicks him in the balls and sends him sprawling, breathless, on the floor.*

JACQUELINE. How about an ending in which I screw you, Director, instead of an ending in which you screw me and everybody else? An ending in which we find out who you really are, what you did to get where you are, an ending in which I strip you naked, and we see the little girls you've pawed, the secretaries you fucked under this desk, the cunts you've forced open with a broomstick, the lives you've ruined, the bribes you've taken, the people you've betrayed.

DIRECTOR. You wanted a different ending, you bitch – you've got it. (*To the* MAN.) You know what to do to her.

MAN. Why are you always calling on me?

DIRECTOR. You think I like this? Doing this? But when you're faced with a plague, when it's already here, contaminating everything . . . After her, who's next? You know how to stop a plague? The only way? (*To* DON ALFONSO *as much as to the* MAN.) You cut off the unhealthy flesh from the body, right, burn everything the wound touched, cleanse it, right, you do it to save the rest of the body. You learn to live with the wound. You learn to forget the wound. Right? Those are the rules. Doesn't she have to live by the rules as we all do? Doesn't she have to face the consequences?

MAN. Yes, I would say she does. I'd say she does have to face the consequences.

The MAN *goes up to* JACQUELINE, *gives her a gag. She takes it with dignity, covers her mouth, is lead to a chair, sits in it. Lights go down on her and the* MAN.

DIRECTOR. These women, my God. Tanya, Sonia, Jacqueline, Irene. It's like a fucking merry-go-round . . . . As for you.

DON ALFONSO. Yes. I am here. You can always count on me.

DIRECTOR. You know what I want.

DON ALFONSO. You want me to write her confession. And forge her name on it.

DIRECTOR. Just like you did with Tanya, yes.

DON ALFONSO. Right. And tomorrow you'll ask me to do it again, right? Again and again and again. Until the day I die. Right? Because this is who I am. This is what I write. This is the life I wrote for myself.

DIRECTOR. Yeah. It's the life you wrote for yourself, Alfonso. So – draft her confession and be done with it. You never loved her anyway. Kill her – just like you killed Daniel Lucas. With the brush of a pen on a piece of paper. With a finger tapping on a machine.

DON ALFONSO *limps across the stage to the typewriter. He sits down in front of it in a closed circle of light.*

DIRECTOR. Good boy.

DON ALFONSO *begins to type. Then he stops.*

DON ALFONSO. Director. I would like – would you answer something?

DIRECTOR. A riddle. I love riddles.

DON ALFONSO *types some more.*

DON ALFONSO. How do you recognise somebody, Director? If you had to choose one thing that – just one thing that makes somebody who he is – what would it be?

DIRECTOR. I don't know what you're getting at.

DON ALFONSO *continues typing.*

DON ALFONSO. Let me put it another way: what do we leave behind when we die?

DIRECTOR. Let's see. Some people leave children.

DON ALFONSO. Children who hate us. What else?

DIRECTOR. Memories.

DON ALFONSO. The harm we did.

DIRECTOR. I really don't understand this sudden negative mood of yours, Alfonso. You've got everything you wanted this morning when you woke up: your son's out of danger, you're the new Director, we're rid of that bitching woman with her boring Thursday evening trysts. And it's all been done without bloodshed: I mean, to murder a character, a fiction, somebody unreal . . .

DON ALFONSO. I didn't.

DIRECTOR. You didn't what?

DON ALFONSO. I didn't murder Daniel Lucas.

DIRECTOR. What do you mean?

DON ALFONSO. Listen.

DON ALFONSO *reads from the paper he has been typing.*

'Daniel knew that he did not have much time. He opened the door to Irene's cell . . . '

DIRECTOR. Give me that confession.

DON ALFONSO. It's not her confession.

Lights go up on IRENE, *blindfolded, torso tied to her chair. DON ALFONSO takes the paper from the typewriter and takes a limping step towards* IRENE, *helping himself with his umbrella.*

DIRECTOR. What do you mean, it's not her – What is it?

DON ALFONSO. Watch and you'll find out.

DON ALFONSO *takes another step. Lights rise on the* MAN.

MAN (*casual, friendly*). If I were you, my man, I'd stop right there.

DON ALFONSO *stops on the edge of the circle of light.*

Didn't I tell you not to fuck with the borders? Isn't that the one piece of friendly advice I've been giving you? Because once you cross the border, once you break down the barriers, step across the line, if you know what I mean – then it's a one-way ticket. There's no going back. It's like – like death.

DON ALFONSO. Or like birth.

MAN. Or like birth, if you want to be more positive, I suppose.

DON ALFONSO. 'Or like birth, Daniel Lucas thought to himself.'

DIRECTOR. What in the hell is this, Alfonso? If you're
  double-crossing me . . . . You know what's going to . . . ?

DON ALFONSO. 'Daniel knew what was going to happen to
  him, he had imagined it too many times to be able to erase
  it from his eyes now as he took the final steps towards the
  one person he was not prepared to betray.'

  DON ALFONSO *takes one more step. He has reached the
  lights that separate him from* IRENE.

DIRECTOR. You can't do this.

DON ALFONSO. 'Daniel knew that he could do this, that he
  could do anything he wanted in this world. That he did not
  need the Director's permission to see Irene.'

DIRECTOR. We'll see about that. (*To the* MAN.) Get him. Get
  him before he –

MAN. We can't touch him. Not yet.

DIRECTOR. What do you mean?

MAN. The rules are the rules. Anybody can tell their story one
  last time.

DIRECTOR. But he's – he's breaking down the barriers, he's
  creating disorder.

MAN. He can do that. As long as he's willing to face the consequences. That's what I'm here for. To make sure everybody
  faces the consequences, everybody plays by the rules.

DIRECTOR. The rules? This man is destroying himself, this
  man I trusted is destroying everything we –

MAN (*cold, blunt*). Don't waste my time. Just say good-bye to
  your friend.

DIRECTOR. You poor bastard. You know what? I'm going to
  miss you. You sonofabitch, I'm going to miss you. To think
  I was worried about your soul.

MAN. The body. That's all there is – one day there's a body.
  The next day, not even a body. But while he's the owner of
  his body, he can fucking well do what he pleases with it.
  Then it's our turn.

DON ALFONSO. When?

MAN. I told you I was your friend.

DON ALFONSO. When is it over?

MAN. Soon. Not much time left. Time to say good-bye. Not much more.

The MAN *and the* DIRECTOR *fade into the shadows on either side of the stage.*

DON ALFONSO. 'Only time for Daniel Lucas to say good-bye.'

DON ALFONSO *lets the umbrella fall and then smiles in a way we have never seen before. He crosses into the other light and stops limping. He has become, this time consciously,* DANIEL LUCAS. *He is, for the first time, entirely himself. The stage is almost bare, a prison.* DANIEL *reaches* IRENE *and squats next to her.*

IRENE. Who is it?

DANIEL *gently takes* IRENE's *hands and places them on his face.*

DANIEL. Do you know what this is?

IRENE. Your face.

DANIEL. No. It's my skull. If I were dead, in the dark, you wouldn't recognise it.

IRENE. I'd recognise you.

DANIEL. Poor child. Out of love you say that, but if my skull lay next to – another man's skull on a dead table, you wouldn't know the difference. Underneath this skin, under this false face – no true self, only unrecognisable bones under the darkness. No, that's not how we recognise each other, that's not the way people should remember each other.

IRENE. You haven't come to save me, have you?

DANIEL. I can't. I'm done with saving people. I can't save anybody anymore.

IRENE. So you've come to say good-bye?

DANIEL. Yes. We've come to say good-bye.

> DANIEL *takes off her blindfold. They look at each other for a few beats. Lights dim on her but do not disappear.* DANIEL *touches her lips gently, rises, turns towards the other side of the stage.* NICK *is tied to a chair, also blindfolded.* DANIEL *walks towards him while* IRENE *watches.*

DANIEL. My boy?

NICK. Dad?

DANIEL. My boy.

NICK. I – if you've come so I can forgive you for –

DANIEL. Shhhh. Don't say anything, my boy. We don't have much time. I want to tell you something. Remember when you were a child and you woke at night and you wanted a story, remember how I would always leave the ending for the next night? Remember? Well – it's the next night now – and that's why I've come. It's time to end this story.

NICK. What story?

DANIEL. You know what story. It's about a man who believed dreams are meaningless, who scratches his head with his hand, a man who limped at times and at times didn't. That story.

NICK. And you've – now you know how it ends?

DANIEL. That's why I'm here. Because I know how it ends.

NICK. So you've read it. Till the end.

DANIEL. I don't need to read it. Not anymore. I'm not a reader anymore. Do you understand?

NICK. No.

DANIEL. Then listen, Nick. In that story, there's a son – his name is – a son who – things don't go very well for him, I'm afraid. Or for his – father.

> DANIEL *unties his son.*

NICK. All of this is in the book . . . This scene, this meeting, we – That means you . . . You released the book.

DANIEL. Yes.

NICK. But nobody will ever read it, nobody will ever . . .

DANIEL. That's not true. That's what they tell us over and over again so we won't write our endings, our own lives. At this very moment, Nick, right now, as we speak, somebody is watching, somebody is hearing us, reading us. Right now.

NICK. And that's all? That's how this ends?

DANIEL. No. There's something missing. Something that hasn't been written yet. Something that the author didn't have time to complete. Are you listening? I want you to add something. It's something your mother would have wanted me to – . Can you do that? For me? For us? As a way of saying – good-bye.

NICK. I can try.

DANIEL. It's something your mother would have liked whispered to her, written on her wall before she died. It's something that comes after the last page of that book. Do you remember the last page?

Sounds of terror approaching. Sirens, dogs, metal bars clattering against iron bars, orders, whispers, curses. Nearer and nearer.

NICK. I remember the last page. When those men start to –

DANIEL. No. Don't. I don't want to know. Are you ready?

NICK. Yes, Dad.

NICK *stands up, barely able to move. Dimly we see the faraway figure of* TANYA *appear, watching, joining* IRENE.

DANIEL. Write this then. This would come after the words: He was finally one person.

NICK. After: He was finally one person.

DANIEL. After the words: The End. That's when this comes.

NICK. After the words: The End. Yes.

The sound of men in boots running towards the stage. The shadowy faces of the MAN *and the* DIRECTOR *emerge from the darkness, their bodies become slowly visible.*

DANIEL. Every book needs an epilogue. Write this down:

As NICK *faces the audience,* DANIEL *painstakingly speaks above the din of the boots coming towards them:*

'Epilogue. Once upon a time . . . '

NICK. 'Once upon a time . . . '

DANIEL. 'Once upon a time there was a man who was afraid . . . '

As DANIEL *speaks and his son echoes him, the* DIRECTOR *and the* MAN *emerge from the shadows and advance upon them. A light on* NICK *remains as he looks out into the audience defiantly.*

NICK. 'Once upon a time there was a man who was afraid.'

Then: black out.

End of play.

Afterword

Reader began life as a short story.

I came to it after having spent many years, like most exiles do, exploring the minds and bodies of the victims of terror, wondering how to give a voice to what was being suppressed back home. A voice and, ultimately, a place on stage: it was that obsession which was to give birth to two other plays of mine. Remember Paulina, the protagonist of *Death and the Maiden*, a woman who, after fifteen years of silence and madness due to her torture as a political prisoner, attempts to force society – through the two men who have power in that society and in her life – to recognise her pain and, indeed, her very existence. She manages a sort of victory in the struggle to have this version of her own life confirmed, though it is made ambiguous by the fractured world of history that she cannot abolish. Another female protagonist, the illiterate and impoverished Sofia Fuentes, in *Widows* has a similar fierce desire not to let the past be buried, not to allow the State to eradicate her family and her memories from the earth.

In *Reader*, for the first time, I wanted to focus on somebody entirely different, someone who, instead of being the captive of terror, is one of the many wheels in the machinery of established power that creates victims, that crushes and forbids the words of others: yes, I invented a censor to live at the core of the story I wanted to tell. Glad to have one of my oppressors in my fictional hands, in my all-too-real hands, I submitted that man to an experiment, the sort of trap Paulina would have gleefully forced on the Doctor, that Sofia would have planned for the Captain if she had found the means to do so. What would happen, I asked, if the book that censor is supposed to ban, turns out to be about him, the past he wants to hide, but also the future he cannot avoid? What if the book begins to come true in front of his eyes? What if he cannot quell his own imagination? What if there is a woman like Paulina, a woman like Sofia, in his past, and she will not be quiet?

As I began to answer these questions, first in the short story and then, over the years, in many drafts and versions of the play, I discovered that *Reader* had depths and dilemmas that went beyond my original idea where an agent of the State has to confront the terrible truth that if you destroy another human being you will end up destroying your own self as well. By forcing the protagonist to face the splits and cracks of his inner world, I also was inevitably probing, as I do in my latest novel *Konfidenz* and my memoir *Heading South, Looking North*, the questions of identity and trust in a world such as ours and asking myself and the audience about the fountains of creativity itself, the role of art in our times. And so the play ended up wondering how stories can be told at the end of this millennium, not only in societies that are miserable enough to suffer dictators, but also in more affluent lands where other more subtle forms of censorship prevail, where a few omnipotent technicolour men in offices decide among themselves what the rest of the populace are going to read and see and hear, in other words, how is reality itself constructed for us and by us and without us, how can we tell what is true and what is false if we do not simultaneously question power, if we have lost our capacity to separate good from evil?

So it is clear that if *Reader* started out as a sort of prankish revenge against the censors who, in Chile, were banning my own work and that of so many other writers, it needed in its newest incarnation to reach audienes in other apparently faraway places. It is a drama that, in some startling sense, like *Death and the Maiden* and like *Widows*, is happening right now, anywhere in the world where lives are being twisted and diminished, where people are trying to take control of their lives and cannot do so until they are willing to see themselves in the mirror of others.

I hope this play, therefore, turns into further proof that my Latin American experience can speak to audiences around the globe, that my literature continues to be a bridge between people and a way of joining them together. But more than that, I have another, more secret, desire: perhaps a hidden censor or

two will read this story, will see this play, will buy this book or
steal it from a lover's house, perhaps he will discover with
horror and wonderment that this is his life, that the truths he
has been trying to suppress are irrepressibly alive in these
pages I wrote for him and myself and everybody else in the
world.